PRAISE FOR JESUS IN THE CO

In a society that is changing rapidly, it is refi... to know that we have a godly man, John Ma...., on the frontlines representing and defending the principles of God that govern the church but that society wants to do away with. *Jesus in the Courtroom* is testimony after testimony of the power of God; it is about His church deciding to stay silent no more and God showing up in the midst of chaos, defending and preserving biblical truth. John is one who, alongside his team, has helped countless pastors and ministries to believe that yes, with God all things are possible, and anyone in ministry who reads this book will be encouraged to not stay silent and also step up to the frontline. Thank you, John, for many years of wise counsel.

Jose Acevedo Jr.
Pastor of Iglesia Monte de Sion

Jesus in the Courtroom gives us powerful insight into God's ultimate purpose for laws, lawyers, judges, and legal systems. It brings understanding to the various ways it impacts our lives. This awesome book shines light upon the great need for intercession and encouragement for those operating in the legal realm.

Arthurine L. Wilkinson
Pastor at Manifest Glory International Ministries

This book speaks to all believers, lawyers, and non-lawyers alike, as citizen-disciples who are called to influence today's culture for Christ. Mauck's keen insights, exemplary legal career, and overflowing compassion combine for compelling advocacy on numerous social, moral, and ultimately spiritual issues our times. His heartening words of encouragements and practical application tools for making a kingdom difference are not to be missed!

Sally Wagenmaker, JD
Founding Attorney of Wagenmaker & Oberly
President-elect, Christian Legal Society National Board Member

God is a God of order as observed in the laws governing His marvelous creation. It would stand to reason that Jesus, as God, would have great insight into the laws governing human affairs. John Mauck's book *Jesus in the Courtroom* shows just how versed Jesus is in the law and justice. This wonderful book will give you a great understanding of the law in Jesus' day, how He was a Master of the law, and that He should be the Master of us all.

Jim Scudder Jr.
President, Dayspring Bible College & Seminary

JESUS
IN THE
COURT
ROOM

How Believers Can Engage the Legal System
for the Good of His World

JOHN W. MAUCK, JD

MOODY PUBLISHERS

CHICAGO

Names in some stories have been changed to protect the privacy of individuals.

All Scripture quotations, unless otherwise indicated, are taken from the Holy Bible, New International Version®, NIV®. Copyright © 1973, 1978, 1984, 2011 by Biblica, Inc.™ Used by permission of Zondervan. All rights reserved worldwide. www.zondervan.com. The "NIV" and "New International Version" are trademarks registered in the United States Patent and Trademark Office by Biblica, Inc.™

Scripture quotations marked ESV are from The Holy Bible, English Standard Version® (ESV®), copyright © 2001 by Crossway, a publishing ministry of Good News Publishers. Used by permission. All rights reserved.

Scripture quotations marked NKJV are taken from the New King James Version. Copyright © 1982 by Thomas Nelson. Used by permission. All rights reserved.

Scripture quotations marked KJV are taken from the King James Version.

Interior Design: Erik M. Peterson
Author Photo: Andrew Collings Photography in Chicago
Cover Design: Faceout Studio
Cover image of Bible: copyright © 2017 by Mega Pixel / Shutterstock (212541577). All rights reserved.
Cover image of judge gavel: copyright © 2017 by Jiri Hera / Shutterstock (174793184). All rights reserved.

All websites and phone numbers listed herein are accurate at the time of publication but may change in the future or cease to exist. The listing of website references and resources does not imply author or publisher endorsement of the site's entire contents. Groups and organizations are listed for informational purposes, and listing does not imply author or publisher endorsement of their activities.

ISBN: 978-0-8024-1515-8

We hope you enjoy this book from Moody Publishers. Our goal is to provide high-quality, thought-provoking books and products that connect truth to your real needs and challenges. For more information on other books and products written and produced from a biblical perspective, go to www.moodypublishers.com or write to:

Moody Publishers
820 N. LaSalle Boulevard
Chicago, IL 60610

1 3 5 7 9 10 8 6 4 2

Printed in the United States of America

To the children whose laughter
would have brought light to our lives.

CONTENTS

FOREWORD

I met John fifteen years ago at a Christian Legal Society national conference. Since that time, I have witnessed firsthand how John is a friend to many, a mentor to some, a great attorney, and a lover of Jesus. You can't know John and not know how much he loves the Lord.

John wrote this book out of a lifelong passion as a Christian lawyer. He is the first named partner of a small law firm in Chicago, but he does not view his firm primarily as a place to practice law. Rather, he sees it as a place from which he can minister to others and be obedient to the Lord's calling on his life.

His law firm website testifies to this: "For me, being a lawyer is about serving God," John writes. "When you do something for a long time it becomes part of who you are—part of your identity." The thing that makes John so genuine is the way he loves others. He does not just minister sitting in his office; he can often be found spending time with those wandering in and out of the courthouse in Chicago, praying with them and caring for them.

John is not just a minister; he is a lawyer, too. And those roles are one in the same for him. The pinnacle of John's law practice is the overwhelming work he does to defend the church. He and his firm work tirelessly to protect churches and ministries from being pushed around by the state. He has appeared in federal, state, and local cases alongside those trying to keep the government at bay. John even helped pass the federal law (RLUIPA—Religious Land Use and Institutionalized Persons Act) he now defends in case after case.

I have spent many a committee and/or board meeting with John. When everyone else wants to talk about procedures or rules, John wants to talk about Jesus. He continuously points people to the Scriptures. He spearheaded the move towards discipleship at the Christian Legal Society, encouraging lawyers and law students to grow in their love for and obedience to Jesus Christ.

Finally, John has a passion for our Jewish neighbors. He and I both miss our mutual friend, Jhan Moskowitz, who was a leader at Jews for Jesus and passed away a few years ago in a tragic accident. Jhan loved others with a depth that few people have. John carries the torch of Jhan like no other person I know. You will see it sprinkled throughout this book.

Jesus in the Courtroom is not really about culture, law, and attorneys. It is really about the One who John represents every time he puts on his tie. John knows who saved him and who he represents before every client, friend, lawyer, and judge. John strives to be "Jesus" in the courtroom, and I think we can all learn from him.

David Nammo
Executive Director and CEO of the Christian Legal Society

INTRODUCTION

For to us a child is born, to us a son is given, and the government will be on his shoulders. And he will be called Wonderful Counselor, Mighty God, Everlasting Father, Prince of Peace.
Isaiah 9:6

Believers today are facing many unique challenges—repression of biblical values, advocacy of abortion, rejection of truth as a transcending paradigm, devastating sexual confusion and behavior, shameful abuse of children and the poor, and rampant hostility toward specific people groups. These challenges manifest themselves not only in the culture at large and in the media, but also in the legal system. Yet we need not despair. Even though many believers do not know how to engage the legal system today, Jesus, our Wonderful Counselor, stands ready to help us understand the seemingly impenetrable and often frustrating areas of God's Law, human law, and lawyers.

Jesus also encountered manifold challenges during His earthly ministry. Many came from the legal and religious systems and leaders of His day. Instead of being discouraged, He used those challenges as opportunities to build God's kingdom. I believe Jesus has set an example for how we can confront the challenges we face today. This book, therefore, explores what it means to be a "citizen-disciple," to be a follower of Jesus who participates in fighting for justice and mercy not only in the culture and society at large, but also in the legal system. Faithful citizenship is part of our discipleship. Jesus cared about the legal realm, and so should we. After all, law—and ultimately God's Law—was given to humanity to promote and maintain human flourishing. Unfortunately, many laws today detract from human flourishing by perpetuating injustice and evil. In this book, you will learn how the assaults on our faith—and ultimately on God's good and perfect Law—not only require us to defend our values, but also afford us incredible opportunities to go on the offense to turn hearts toward truth, to explain the unseen God, and to advance His kingdom. It's possible to win these battles—whether at the Supreme Court or at a local city council.

Isaiah 9:6 communicates a profound truth relevant to believers in every land and every time. As you read this book, you will discover that the Wonderful Counselor promised long ago is not only a spiritual guide, but also a legal adviser, a lawyer, an advocate, an extraordinary strategist. As Jesus taught God's Law, He not only provided an accurate understanding of God's Law, but also modeled how that understanding should both *inform* and *reform* human law. He is "Jesus in the courtroom."

The Bible tells us Jesus is returning—perhaps tomorrow, perhaps in the next millennium. In the meantime, we must prepare ourselves and help the world prepare for that event through acts of justice and mercy, with a firm dedication to sharing the gospel. Satan will surely attack us and our efforts, and will try to thwart the Messiah's return. This book, and ultimately Jesus Himself, will show us ways to engage both God's Law and human law to defeat Satan and evil—and win the hearts of some who now hate the Light.

Because law is so critical to many of the challenges against truth that we face today, I have used my experiences as a religious liberty attorney and insights as a Bible scholar to help us see how all believers, not just lawyers, can influence the seemingly mysterious realm of law to work for and redeem our society. While I write as an American attorney in the twenty-first century, I hope that most of the problems addressed and solutions offered in *Jesus in the Courtroom* will transcend cultures and time. While we will certainly visit what happens in actual courtrooms and in lawsuits, we will go beyond to meet lawyers, judges, children, churches, and others in pursuit of God's justice so that we may better understand how law affects every area of human life and how each of us can be an effective citizen-disciple. Along the way, you will be introduced to many ways in which the legal tools and biblical-spiritual arsenal that God has given us can be combined effectively to this end.

After graduating from the University of Chicago Law School, I began practice in 1972, concentrating primarily in real estate. In 1985, I received a distinct call from God to engage in zoning litigation for churches. After learning how to apply constitutional principles to land use, my practice, in partnership with other believing attorneys, has grown to represent clients in the areas of religious liberty, free speech, and defense of life. In the process, God has taught me essential lessons on how to achieve kingdom objectives. I also wrote the award-winning *Paul on Trial* (Thomas Nelson, 2001), which argues that the book of

Acts was written originally as a legal brief to defend Paul as he awaited trial before Nero. There you will find legal and biblical scholarship throughout.

Jesus in the Courtroom addresses our engagement on both individual and corporate levels, emphasizing how our respective individual calls from God coalesce into in an effective collective response to the trials we face. Jesus taught us to pray, "Our Father . . . . Thy kingdom come" (Matt. 6:9–10 KJV). In this book, I aim to help you understand what answer to that prayer looks like in the legal realm. In so doing, I also intend to help you develop—if you do not already have one—a healthy attitude toward law, lawyers, and others in various legal contexts, especially those affected by oppression, abortion, child exploitation, and unbiblical sexual ethics. Then, with assurance from our Wonderful Counselor, you will be offered new strategies to address those and other challenges to bring the gospel to our hurting nations.

We begin with insights showing how the Gospels reveal Jesus' plan to influence the lawyers and politicians of Israel during His earthly life and ministry. As I was completing the proposal to Moody Publishers for this book, I happened to meet Wayne Grudem, a leading evangelical theologian and author of *Politics According to the Bible*, by being seated next to him at a family-values breakfast. I explained to him one of the themes of this book: that the Pharisees and Sadducees with whom Jesus interacted and debated should be thought of primarily as lawyers instead of merely as religious leaders. Operating within the scope of Jewish Law—Torah—these religious leaders were also lawmakers, judges, law professors, and politicians. With this fresh perspective, we will more fully understand Jesus' ministry to Israel. Grudem immediately encouraged this approach by commenting how understanding the intense involvement of the Pharisees and Sadducees with the Law would increase our awareness of the number of verses that could give insight into our twenty-first century world of politics and law.

Understanding Jesus' love of Torah and His engagement with legal and political professionals of His day will enable us to better cooperate with our Wonderful Counselor, God's Son. Looking at the Gospels through a legal lens, we will see new ways that love for and strategic engagement with the legal system can bless our lives and our nations.

The word translated as "Counselor" in Isaiah 9:6, from the root word *yâ'ats* in Hebrew, means "to advise, consult, counsel." And that word certainly has legal connotations. The same word is used for "counselors" in Isaiah 1:26: "I will restore your judges as at the first, and your counselors as at the beginning. Afterward you shall be called the city of righteousness, the faithful city" (Isa. 1:26 NKJV). Because Isaiah used *yâ'ats* in context with "judges" and "city of righteousness," we can confidently appreciate and celebrate the legal implications of Isaiah 9:6 and what it says about the promised Messiah, the Wonderful Counselor, who may also be thought of as our Extraordinary Strategist. But even more is packed into that powerful title, as we shall discover.

In every age, God challenges His followers to love and serve Him in the midst of trials, to confront and overcome evil. In the twenty-first century, He has placed believers throughout the world in times of trouble when many laws impose evil. Our Extraordinary Strategist wants us not only to better understand law, the legal system, and how He relates to it, but also to defeat evil and impact the nations with the awesome message of God's mercy. He will help us become defenders, rescuers, and restorers for the abused and wounded.

Included in our trials is the social decay that inevitably results from the rejection of God and His truth. These trials have grown to international scope. Refugee crises seem to affect more and more nations. World leaders appear ineffectual. I believe God is summoning the citizen-disciple to step forward and fill the moral vacuum created by the abandonment of truth and by the legal chaos created as rebellious humanity has purported to displace God as the ultimate source of authority.

Paul wrote to the believers in Rome, "Let everyone be subject to the governing authorities, for there is no authority except that which God has established. The authorities that exist have been established by God" (Rom. 13:1). In America and other democracies at least, the authority in place means neither local nor state government, nor the president, nor federal law, but "we the people" who have ordained and established the constitution. Thus, in a democracy, the people—the citizens—are responsible under God to adopt, and, when necessary, reform laws to reflect God's love of mercy and justice. Disciples of Jesus have a special responsibility because of the multitude of spiritual resources Jesus has available for us. *Jesus in the Courtroom* gives us the opportunity to open our hearts to the numerous practical ways that we can use those gifts in the legal realm. And I hope you will be encouraged and energized when you see the number and power of the spiritual weapons and legal tools God has made available to us.

As we understand better the work of our Wonderful Counselor, Jesus in the courtroom, we will gain a clearer vision for how to move forward in fighting for justice and mercy. Let's start the journey.

CHAPTER 1

WOE TO YOU LAWYERS?

We all can point to many spheres of life in which believers are regularly active, seeking to make an impact for the kingdom—business, media, entertainment, education, sports, medicine, global aid, and more. While many of these areas of human endeavor overlap with law, many believers tend to shy away from engaging the law, even though it is critical to the advancement of truth in our world. Why are we not engaging the law to a greater degree?

One answer is lawyers. Some people do not love the law because they do not love the law's most visible proponents: attorneys and politicians. Others fear the law because they do not understand how the legal system works, or simply because the idea of judgment in general scares them. And are not lawyers wicked? Does not Jesus' statement "Woe to you lawyers!" (NKJV) sum it up for all lawyers for all time?

American history provides much ammunition against lawyers. Consider *Roe v. Wade* in which seven of the nine US Supreme Court justices approved abortion, which legalized the killing of millions of children by wiping out the protection provided by law in fifty states. Justice Byron White, one of the two dissenters, wrote:

> The Court simply fashions and announces a new constitutional right for pregnant mothers and, with scarcely any reason or authority for its action, invests that right with sufficient substance to override most existing state abortion statutes. The upshot is that the people and the legislatures of the 50 States are constitutionally disentitled to weigh the relative importance of the continued existence and development of the fetus, on the one hand, against a spectrum of possible impacts on the mother, on the other hand.[1]

Justice White goes on to call the decision "an exercise of raw judicial power."[2] As a result of the ruling by the Court, woe upon woe has been inflicted upon unborn children, young mothers, America, and probably the justices themselves. Yet in contrast to the woe from Jesus, consider that two justices dissented in *Roe v. Wade* and also that lawmakers, including many lawyers across the fifty states, had first erected protections of unborn children. Not all lawyers deserve opprobrium.

In the US Constitution, the evil of slavery was institutionalized by counting slaves as three-fifths a person. In the 1857 US Supreme Court *Dred Scott v. Sandford* decision, a runaway slave was forced to return to his master.

In 2016, the United Nations Educational, Scientific and Cultural Organization (UNESCO) approved a motion to annul Israel's claim to its holiest site, the Temple Mount, as well as the Western Wall and the Old City of Jerusalem. Whether this resolution is law or a harbinger of law (see Zech. 12:3), the point is that a political agenda created a legal rationale for coercion by purporting to "annul" a claim and "authorize" violence. In legal systems that are based on truth and justice, litigants are allowed to make claims, and competing or conflicting claims are allowed. This resolution regarding the Temple Mount and the Old City appears to be an attempt to subvert the truth by making a law that rewrites history. Anyone who reads the Bible can see Israel indeed has a valid historical claim to these sites and that city. In these three examples, we see that law is a tool that can be wielded for good or evil.

Many Christians join Jesus in proclaiming woe upon lawyers. But that one particular statement that Jesus made does not sum up what all of Scripture teaches about law and lawyers. Why do we have in the Bible Psalm 119, the longest psalm, which extols God's Law for 176 verses? Consider verses 18–20: "Open my eyes that I may see wonderful things in your law. I am a stranger on earth; do not hide your commands from me. My soul is consumed with longing for your laws at all times." If we are to love God's Law, it means that we should love those who handed down God's Law as well. Think about these three men, who functioned in many ways as lawyers:

- Moses, the Law giver
- Paul, the Pharisee/lawyer
- Luke, the doctor turned legal brief writer when he wrote Acts as a defense for Paul's upcoming trial before Nero

All three were key builders of God's kingdom. Apparently God found something in their legal work that could be utilized in their ministries.[3] Moses, Luke, and Paul wrote significant portions of the Bible. Jesus—who rightly interpreted and taught the Law handed down from Moses, who commissioned Paul, and who, as the Word of God, inspired Luke by the power of His Spirit—is not against all law. Nor is His woe directed to all lawyers or even to all law professors, "teachers of the law," whom He repeatedly excoriates in Matthew 23. As Paul explicitly emphasized, "The law is holy, and the commandment is holy, righteous and good" (Rom. 7:12). While Jesus does not oppose the Law per se, neither does He suggest that all laws are good simply because someone with power has promulgated them. Jesus' warning is directed toward those who *misuse* their legal authority to put heavy burdens on others. He exclaims, "They tie up heavy, cumbersome loads and put them on other people's shoulders, but they themselves are not willing to lift a finger to move them" (Matt. 23:4). How, then, are we to discern which laws, lawyers, and legal systems are good, are of God? How should we, both non-lawyers and lawyers, relate to the legal realm? As we pursue those questions, let me introduce you anew to a law professor you already know.

RABBI YESHUA

Christians often tell me they have heard sermons on how Jesus taught, disputed, or otherwise related to the religious leaders of His day. Those sermons and the prevailing Christian understanding of the Gospels are usually incomplete and, in important ways, often mistaken about Jesus' interactions with the Pharisees and Sadducees. So we may be empowered to follow Jesus more faithfully, we must address that confusion and rehear our Rabbi's teaching in its Jewish-legal context.

AT THE TIME OF JESUS, *RABBI* MEANT "TEACHER"— THAT IS, A TEACHER OF THE LAW.

The title *Rabbi* can confuse the modern reader who thinks of a rabbi primarily as a leader of a synagogue. At the time, rabbis were scholars who studied and taught Torah, Israel's Law, but as far as we can tell, they were not generally functioning as "pastors" or synagogue leaders (see Acts 13:15; 18:8 which refer to "leaders of the synagogue," not "rabbis"). And of course, ancient Israel combined government and religion in many ways differently from the ways modern cultures separate aspects of religion and government. However, as we shall discover, similarities abound between first-century rabbis and our modern-day "teachers of the law"—law professors. Not only that, the *Talmidim Yeshua* ("disciples of Jesus") bear important similarities to today's law students. In Acts 22:3, Paul—an apostle and evangelist—chose to list his first credentials to his fellow Jews as being a student of one of the best law professors in Israel: "I studied under Gamaliel and was thoroughly trained in the law of our ancestors." How can we, today's disciples of Jesus, be better disciples by thinking of ourselves as law students? Part of their training in God's Law was preparation for them to make disciples themselves. Is that how we, lawyers and non-lawyers alike, should think about ourselves as we seek to be fully equipped citizen-disciples?

The "religious leaders" and the "religious system" of biblical Israel—both in the first century and before—certainly involved the Levitical priesthood, sacrificial practices, and the temple. Yet the Sadducees and Pharisees, while in some ways being "religious" leaders, were actually more what we today would call lawyers, lawmakers, judges, or politicians. While the large majority of believers today see the Bible primarily as a religious book, the Law or Torah—here defined as the Five Books of Moses, the Prophets, and the Writings—was seen during Jesus' day as the "Constitution" of Israel: the written expressions of how God's people were to live as a society and nation. The Great Sanhedrin—which tried and convicted Jesus, and then handed Him over to Pilate for execution—was the chief tribunal of Jerusalem. Further, under first-century governing practice, every community in Israel with 120 men as heads of families was eligible for self-governance and its own small Sanhedrin (a council). Hundreds of such city councils, village councils, local courts governed by Torah existed throughout Israel during Jesus' day. As we have noted, Paul was a law student under a law professor (rabbi) named Gamaliel. If the Jewish leaders with whom Jesus interacted were more lawyers and judges than the religious leaders we have thought them to be, what implications result?

First, we learn that Jesus, the Extraordinary Strategist, worked to reform legal systems and teachings during His own day. When we realize this, we begin to see that Jesus' plan to bless humanity contains significant forensic dimensions. This broadened awareness should open our hearts and minds to new paths down which we can walk with the Savior. And after appreciation comes appropriation. The more we learn about the legal aspects of Jesus' ministry, the more equipped we are to engage the law and legal systems in our own day.

Let's step back for a moment. Jesus came to a fallen world. To redeem it, He used what real estate investors call "leverage." Rather than be born into, say, a Viking community, the Savior incarnated amid a people with a long history of interacting with the Creator. The Jews had a well-developed understanding of sin, repentance, and atonement. They had the Hebrew Bible and a longing and expectation for the Messiah. Could Jesus have reached the world as effectively using Norsemen? Were Anders or Erick qualified to write the Gospels or the letter to the Hebrews? Of course not!

To impact the world for God's kingdom, Jesus came to God's people, the Jews. Jesus Himself said, "I was sent only to the lost sheep of Israel" (Matt. 15:24). He chose to multiply, to leverage, His teaching by entrusting it to disciples who were qualified to teach others (2 Tim. 2:2). Concomitantly, to reach Israel, Jesus focused on teaching and living Torah with twelve men and other disciples while educating, challenging, and provoking to jealousy the legal establishment. This brilliant strategy will become clearer as we focus on how the Gospels underscore Jesus' priority to explain the Law and to impact the legal professionals and systems of His day.

THE TRUE TEACHER OF THE LAW

Let us consider in more detail not only that Jesus sought to impact the legal system of His day, but also that He did so *as a lawyer*. Consider a familiar passage, which is essentially a first-century equivalent of a "law faculty" debate:

> The Pharisees got together. One of them, an expert in the law, tested him with this question: "Teacher, which is the greatest commandment in the Law?"
> Jesus replied: "'Love the Lord your God with all your heart and with all your soul and with all your mind.' This is the first and greatest commandment. And the second is like it: 'Love your neighbor as yourself.' All the Law and the Prophets hang on these two commandments." (Matt. 22:34–40)

Here we see Jesus teaching other lawyers the true meaning of the Law and its ultimate purpose. He was, to put it simply, revealing to them, and us, the two most important, most fundamental provisions of the law—to love God and our neighbors. As Moses declared long ago, "The Lord your God will raise for you a prophet like me from among you, from you fellow Israelites. You must listen to him" (Deut. 18:15).

While Moses specifically mentions a *prophet*, he did not simply mean a figure who would come to reveal the future. While prophets of Israel certainly did that from time to time, they were essentially teachers. They revealed who God was, taught His Law, and called people to live in accordance with what God had revealed—that is, His Law. The gospel reveals time and again that Jesus is the true Prophet—not only the one whom the Torah anticipates as the Savior of the world, but also the one who perfectly understands and teaches God's Law.

In order to more fully understand how Jesus functioned as a lawyer and to demystify legal analysis for some of you who find it intimidating, we will consider three simple principles of legal analysis.

Principle 1: Conflicting Laws

Approach:

- Ask whether the laws really conflict or whether they can be harmonized
- If they truly conflict, determine which law takes priority and why (for example, a provision of the US Constitution takes precedence over a Chicago zoning ordinance)

Strategy: prioritize

Principle 2: Ambiguous Laws

Approach:

- For truth seekers—resolve ambiguity by discerning the intent of the originator of the law (God, legislature, etc.)
- For ideologues—ignore context and history of law and twist the law to fit one's ideology

Strategy: harmonize by using intent to eliminate ambiguity

Principle 3: Harsh Result of Law

Approach:

- Determine whether law as applied is socially counterproductive
- If it is, mediate law's effect through pardon, commutation, amendment, or procedural challenge

Strategy: humanize

With these three simple principles and God's overarching commands listed in Matthew 22:36–40 in mind, we will consider three instances in which Rabbi Yeshua applies these principles to help others see the true meaning of God's Law, to do good to others, and to honor God.

Our first example, from Mark 2:23–27, shows Jesus functioning, in effect, as a defense lawyer-advocate for His students:

> One Sabbath Jesus was going through the grainfields, and as his disciples walked along, they began to pick some heads of grain. The Pharisees said to him, "Look, why are they doing what is unlawful on the Sabbath?"
>
> He answered, "Have you never read what David did when he and his companions were hungry and in need? In the days of Abiathar the high priest, he entered the house of God and ate the consecrated bread, which is lawful only for priests to eat. And he also gave some to his companions."
>
> Then he said to them, "The Sabbath was made for man, not man for the Sabbath." (Mark 2:23–27)

In defending His disciples, Jesus applies the first two of the above principles. First, He addressed the apparent conflict (Principle 1) between the fourth commandment establishing the Sabbath and the Pharisaic traditions that sharply restricted human activity on the Sabbath. Jesus implicitly asserts the primacy of Exodus 20:8 (the Sabbath command) over those Pharisaic traditions. He prioritized. He also implicitly asserted that if there was any question of whether the Pharisaic traditions conflicted with Exodus 20:8 (Principle 2), the question was best resolved by considering the purpose of the law (to give man rest, not more burdens) and the character of God the Lawmaker (who is gracious and encouraging, not tyrannical). He harmonized.

In our second example, Jesus addresses a rabbinical debate over marriage and divorce, and Deuteronomy 24:1 in particular: "If a man marries a woman who becomes displeasing to him because he finds something indecent about her, and he writes her a certificate of divorce, gives it to her and sends her from his house [and she marries another man, the first husband may not subsequently remarry her]." Rabbis argued over the meaning of "becomes displeasing" and "finds something indecent." One rabbinic school of interpretation held that if a woman did something equivalent to burning the toast or forgetting to pay the phone bill, then her husband could send her away because she was "displeasing." Of course, this interpretation would leave women subject to arbitrary harsh treatment by their husbands and thus in great danger. The school of "law professor" Rabbi Shammai understood "becomes displeasing" and "finds something indecent about her" as a euphemism for adultery.

With that background information, consider how Jesus answered the question in Matthew 19 posed by other law professors:

> "Is it lawful for a man to divorce his wife for any and every reason?"

"Haven't you read," he replied, "that at the beginning the Creator 'made them male and female,' and said, 'For this reason a man will leave his father and mother and be united to his wife, and the two will become one flesh'? So they are no longer two, but one flesh. Therefore what God has joined together, let no one separate."

"Why then," they asked, "did Moses command that a man give his wife a certificate of divorce and send her away?"

Jesus replied, "Moses permitted you to divorce your wives because your hearts were hard. But it was not this way from the beginning. I tell you that anyone who divorces his wife, except for sexual immorality, and marries another woman commits adultery." (vv. 3–9)

In this scenario, Jesus resolves the ambiguity in Deuteronomy 24:1. (I believe God gave some ambiguous laws and other ambiguous Scriptures for the same reason He gave Israel an "incomplete" law—which we will discuss in detail in the next section—so we could learn to apply unambiguous laws and truths in godly ways.) Jesus explains that the divorce law must be understood in light of the broader context of Scripture:

- Principle 1: Yeshua first teaches the fundamental importance of marriage as an institution created by God. Jesus prioritized.

- Principle 2: To resolve the scriptural ambiguity, Jesus addresses man's fallenness/sinfulness/hardness-of-heart in context with the purposes of God, the merciful Lawgiver (see Ex. 34:5–7). Jesus harmonized.

- Principle 3: Using the first two principles, Jesus mediated the harsh result of putting the woman on the street. Jesus humanized.

Our final example shows the time Jesus functioned perhaps most memorably as both a defense attorney and a judge, when He was confronted with a woman who merited death by stoning according to the Torah:

> At dawn he appeared again in the temple courts, where all the people gathered around him, and he sat down to teach them. The teachers of the law and the Pharisees brought in a woman caught in adultery. They made her stand before the group and said to Jesus, "Teacher, this woman was caught in the act of adultery. In the Law Moses commanded us to stone such women. Now what do you say?" They were using this question as a trap, in order to have a basis for accusing him.
>
> But Jesus bent down and started to write on the ground with his finger. When they kept on questioning him, he straightened up and said to them, "Let any one of you who is without sin be the first to throw a stone at her." Again he stooped down and wrote on the ground.
>
> At this, those who heard began to go away one at a time, the older ones first, until only Jesus was left, with the woman still standing there. Jesus straightened up and asked her, "Woman, where are they? Has no one condemned you?"
>
> "No one, sir," she said.
>
> "Then neither do I condemn you," Jesus declared. "Go now and leave your life of sin." (John 8:2–11)

In John 8, no conflict of law (Principle 1) or ambiguity (Principal 2) exists, but the application of the law would have a harsh result (Principal 3). In fact, the teachers of the Law and the Pharisees were trying to trap Jesus. For they brought only the woman forward when the Law commands that both the adulterous man and woman should be put to death (Lev. 20:10; Deut. 22:22). Because of their motives, they were probably malicious witnesses, as referenced in Deuteronomy 19:16–19, and therefore incurred upon themselves the punishment of death by stoning. Thus, Jesus as a legal defender/advocate leads the woman's accusers to disqualify themselves as witnesses. Then, speaking in a judicial manner, He pardons her.

JUSTICE AND MERCY

These above scenarios not only teach us that Jesus functioned as a lawyer, advocate, and judge, but also reinforce that the ultimate purpose of the Law, or Torah, is to lead humans to love both God and neighbor. The lawyers of Jesus' day had lost sight of this. They placed burdens on people that prevented human flourishing and in so doing dishonored God. Jesus, therefore, acted as a legal reformer. He wanted Israel and its leaders to understand that Torah—which is not simply the Ten Commandments or the first five books of the Bible, but rather all of Scripture—reveals God as a God of justice and mercy who loves His world. Additionally, the Bible shows us that God gave us His laws to protect society, families, and individuals. By giving His Law to protect society and help it function well, He teaches morality, showing us the differences between right and wrong, good and evil. That much is clear in commands such as "You shall not murder" and "You shall not commit adultery" (Ex. 20:13–14). Or consider the beautiful gift of sexuality, which God gave to married couples to enjoy and so they may become creators like Him through the procreation of little ones. However, this gift was so potent that God put limits—laws—on it to protect humans from abusing their sexuality. He also gave those limits because He loves us and wants the best for us and our society. Not only that, He gives us the strength to live within those limits.

Yet God's Law does not address all circumstances. In a sense, it is incomplete. How? Some of the issues it addresses transcend all times and cultures, yet other issues were particular to Israel, and the surrounding nations. Just as one size of a garment cannot fit all people and usually cannot accommodate most, so the Law doesn't address all issues for all times. This is not to say that the Torah is unhelpful. The Hebrew Scriptures contain many accounts of human moral failure and success, examples of right and wrong that still guide us today. From Cain and Abel to Joseph to Gideon to Ruth to David to Esther—these narratives were given to teach the Jews, and eventually the Gentiles, how they should live and govern themselves. And these narratives and decrees set forth precedents and principles that can be emulated and applied in different contexts. Consider the account about judges, where Jethro, Moses's father-in-law, urges him to train and delegate to other qualified men the task of resolving disputes (Ex. 18:17–23). This would both relieve Moses of the weight of too many responsibilities and help equip others to administer God's justice and, through explanation of the reasons for a particular decision, educate the people about God, justice, and mercy. One principle we can draw from this is that humans need qualified leaders, and that leaders need to delegate tasks to others because they cannot carry every burden themselves.

Micah 6:8 sums up rather succinctly the open-ended purpose of the "incomplete" Law: "What does the LORD require of you? To act justly and to love mercy and to walk humbly with your God." I believe God's intended goal for the legal systems of the nations—their constitutions, laws, and legal decisions—parallels the reason He gave Torah to Israel: that they would exemplify God's justice and mercy. But laws are made by humans, and when men and women forget to walk humbly with God, the laws often do not reflect His character. Such people can be deceived into creating laws that oppress and exploit others because they have neglected, been oblivious to, or disobeyed Torah. In other cases, they simply want to make themselves the ultimate decider of right and wrong. As Law professor Paul wrote, the Law is good *if* used properly (1 Tim. 1:8).

The Law gives humans a measurement for their own conduct. Such standards inform us that we all have fallen short of right conduct, even right attitude, and that we need God's help. That is why God sent the Messiah. Paul writes, "When I understood the commandment 'you shall not covet,' the commandment gave the opportunity to my sinful nature to produce in me all kinds of covetous desire" (Rom. 7:7–9, my paraphrase). He was only potentially covetous before, but when the command came, a dormant covetousness sprang to life. Then Paul goes on to explain that the Law was good because it helped him see his need for a Savior, the Messiah!

But what about people who don't believe in the Bible or maybe never have even heard of it? We all know people who reject the Bible, reject good "secular" law, and even some who go so far as to reject the very idea of truth as a transcendent reality. Others go even further by hating or instinctively rebelling against all law. They don't want anyone else telling them what to do or to clean up the messes they have made. Nevertheless, almost everyone has values of some sort, even if they say, "Your values, your God's values, and your society's values are not my values!" But a life committed to living for truth regardless of the cost will find that Messiah Jesus, the Wonderful Counselor, is the one true path to life. And those who follow Him know that God's justice is perfect and that when we sin against His laws, His mercy is available. What amazing grace! But Jesus not only forgives law-breakers; He embodies God's Law perfectly as well, showing us what justice and mercy really look like.

HEEDING COUNSEL

At this point in our journey, I trust you have begun to appreciate the legal aspects of Jesus' ministry to Israel in His days on earth. He acted as a law professor and advocate, who strategically taught, rebuked, corrected, and debated the lawyers, judges, law students, politicians, and law professors of His day.

Yet He is not our only Counselor. Jesus Himself said in John 14 and 16 that the Holy Spirit is also our Advocate/Counselor. On the night He was betrayed, Jesus promised His disciples, "I will ask the Father, and he will give you another advocate to help you and be with you forever" (14:16). He also said, "But the Advocate, the Holy Spirit, whom the Father will send in my name, will teach you all things and will remind you of everything I have said to you" (14:26). He further stated that when "he, the Spirit of truth, comes, he will guide you into all the truth" (16:13). Scripture teaches us that both Jesus and the Holy Spirit are teachers of Torah, God's Law. When Jesus said that He was going to send another "Counselor" or "Advocate," He was saying that the Spirit would continue much of the same ministry that Jesus Himself conducted while on earth, and that He would be with us and in us during Jesus' physical absence. And as Jesus' disciples, His Law students, we carry on His ministry by the power of the Holy Spirit, our other Counselor.

So what exactly is our role? As we citizen-disciples seek to advance God's kingdom through engagement in our legal systems, we need to be certain that we ourselves are becoming active, discerning receivers and followers of the Holy Spirit's counsel. He is the Spirit of truth, and faithful disciples will be receptive to His teaching. This means that we will seek to understand as best as we can both God's Law and godly human law so that we, like Jesus did, can effectively fight for justice and mercy. In order to become informed students of God's Law, we must study His Word, Torah, submit to it, and embody it. One practical way to be informed students of godly human law is to seek to understand it as best as we can. One way to do this is to develop the traits of a good legal client toward our advocate/lawyer Jesus that will help equip us to get into the fray, legally speaking, and ultimately become better citizen-disciples:

- trusts his or her attorney
- is teachable, humble, willing to listen
- is truthful and candid, even when the truth is embarrassing
- has a clear objective that is good, godly
- has a perspective beyond self-interest
- is realistic, will face consequences, and recognizes his or her own weaknesses
- will not push his or her attorney to unethical actions
- prays for or with his or her attorney
- is courageous in standing for truth

I realize that this is easier said than done. In order to become faithful citizen-disciples who fight for justice and mercy, let us be receptive to the work of the Holy Spirit by turning our hearts to God's Law and to God's lawyers. In doing so, we will be better equipped and will learn effective strategies to win the battles we face today and to win souls.

CHAPTER 2

TURNING HEARTS TOWARD GOD'S LAW—AND GOD'S LAWYERS

If we want to help others, we must first turn our hearts to God. One of the best ways to do this is to turn to His Word, Torah. And Torah—the entire Bible—is an expression of who God is and a revelation of how He wants our world to function.

When we realize more deeply how God wants His love, justice, and mercy to suffuse our society, we begin to see the integral part that the teaching of Torah plays in advancing His kingdom. We recall that Jesus was the true faithful Teacher of the Law, and as His disciples, we are called to teach God's Law as well (see Matt. 28:19). Many believers, however, do not love the Law, believing it is irrelevant for today. Yet we are wise to remember that Jesus loved the Law and came not to abolish it, but to fulfill it (Matt. 5:17).

Ask yourself whether you have the attitudes and behaviors listed in Psalm 119. Are you obedient? Have you hidden God's Word in your heart? Do you delight in God's Law? Do you meditate on it frequently?

How do we cultivate such wonderful attitudes toward the

Law and law in general? Some people just seem to have the right attitude toward law, and they love to obey it. Of course, all of us are naturally rebellious in numerous ways. Many of us find all concepts of law—divine or human—boring or even annoying. Yet some people are naturally enthusiastic about God's Law and godly human law.

Having the right attitude about law—and God's Law in particular—is not a passive matter. We should discern how God wants us to relate to His Law and ask the Holy Spirit, the Counselor that Jesus promised to send us, to create in us godly attitudes toward the Law, godly human law, and lawyers. Let this be our prayer: "Dear Father, in reading Psalm 119, I see many ways I fall short of the attitudes you want me to have, specifically [express your particular need(s)]. Please send the Wonderful Counselor to give me the right heart."

Another way to cultivate these attitudes is to consider the role God's Law and lawyers have played in restoring the nation of Israel after the Babylonian exile.

GOD'S LAW AND REVIVAL

One of the most profound revivals of all time occurred in Jerusalem in 444 BC. It centered on God's Law and is recounted in Nehemiah 8:2–12. Nehemiah, after describing how Ezra and others read from the Law all morning, tells us:

> Then Nehemiah the governor, Ezra the priest and teacher of the Law, and the Levites who were instructing the people said to them all, "This day is holy to the LORD your God. Do not mourn or weep." For all the people had been weeping as they listened to the words of the Law.
>
> Nehemiah said, "Go and enjoy choice food and sweet

drinks, and send some to those who have nothing prepared. This day is holy to our Lord. Do not grieve, for the joy of the Lord is your strength." . . .

Then all the people went away to eat and drink, to send portions of food and to celebrate with great joy, because they now understood the words that had been made known to them. (vv. 9–10, 12)

God brought restoration to Israel through the Law in the time of Ezra and Nehemiah. We know that He "is the same yesterday and today and forever" (Heb. 13:8). But, of course, we cannot simply conclude that God built His kingdom through law 2,500 years ago and that maybe He will do so again today if we simply pray enough. Rather, wisdom behooves us to examine more deeply:

- the heart attitudes of the people of Israel;
- their circumstances;
- the actions of their leaders; and
- God's sovereignty.

We will delve into those categories to see what God may be teaching us from them that may apply in our times.

WHAT THE PEOPLE DID

We note that the people assembled at dawn in Nehemiah 8— not just the men, but "the men and women and all who were able to understand" (v. 2). Because the Feast of Trumpets had commenced at the previous sunset, most people probably went to sleep with the hopes from the sound of the trumpets echoing in their hearts. Then as the day dawned, the trumpets' call to assemble may have awakened the people's hearts and spirits to ready themselves to encounter God. The text recounts in detail how they prepared, which certainly must have helped soften their hearts. We read that they even had their teenagers up before dawn and at the meeting! And we know that hearing God's Law read convicted them of their sin, both personal and corporate, because they wept. These were not tears of joy but of mourning, brokenness, and repentance (vv. 9–10). The music, probably a cascade of shofars (see Num. 29:1), not only at the previous sunset and dawn, but also throughout the day, undoubtedly touched their hearts.

HOW THE CIRCUMSTANCES HELPED

Israel had recently returned from seventy years in exile. No doubt, the exile had chastened the people of Israel, making them aware of their neglect of Torah. The restoration prophesied by Jeremiah (25:11–12) and recently fulfilled was undoubtedly fresh in the people's hearts as a concrete demonstration of God's mercy and faithfulness. Consider Psalm 126:

> When the LORD restored the fortunes of Zion,
>   we were like those who dreamed.
> Our mouths were filled with laughter,
>   our tongues with songs of joy.
> Then it was said among the nations.
>   "The LORD has done great things for them."
> The LORD has done great things for us,
>   and we are filled with joy.
> Restore our fortunes, LORD,
>   like streams in the Negev.
> Those who sow with tears
>   will reap with songs of joy.
> Those who go out weeping,

>   carrying seed to sow,
> will return with songs of joy,
>   carrying sheaves with them.

Temple sacrifice had been restored, and the wall had just been rebuilt (Neh. 6:15). Hostile neighboring nations continued to pose a threat to Israel's safety. Then the revival breakthrough occurred on the Feast of Trumpets, possibly the first time the entire community had celebrated this festival since their return from the Babylonian exile. As Numbers 29:1 instructs, "On the first day of the seventh month hold a sacred assembly and do no regular work. It is a day for you to sound the trumpets." Recognizing the miracle of their restoration and how the prophet Isaiah had connected it to the sound of a "great trumpet" surely stirred the nation's heart as they experienced the fulfillment of Isaiah's prophecy:

> In that day the LORD will thresh from the flowing Euphrates to the Wadi of Egypt, and you, Israel, will be gathered up one by one. And in that day a great trumpet will sound. Those who were perishing in Assyria and those who were exiled in Egypt will come and worship the LORD on the holy mountain in Jerusalem. (Isa. 27:12–13)

WHAT THE LEADERS DID

Upon returning from exile, the leaders took a number of concrete actions to demonstrate their worship of God and submission to His authority. They scheduled an assembly to meet at dawn. They prepared by building a high wooden platform, large enough to support at least fourteen men. They exhibited to the congregation God's authority and the authority of His Law through the construction of and their presence on the dais.

They provided supplemental instruction. The people probably had not received much instruction in the Law during the Babylonian exile. Undoubtedly, Ezra read in Hebrew, and although Hebrew had been Israel's language prior to the exile roughly seventy years earlier and was still used or at least understood by most Jews, the Aramaic spoken in Babylon likely weakened the familiarity that some Jews had with Hebrew.

Most crucially, I believe, the leaders did not offer premature or false comfort for violation of the Law. Instead they let the words read by Ezra and the severity of legal transgression take full effect. Apparently, interspersed explanation from the Levites and continued reading by Ezra continued until godly sorrow manifested in mourning and weeping, sometime about midday (see Neh. 8:9–11). Then in unanimity, the leaders all emphasized the holiness of the day to the Lord and exhorted them to rejoice, "enjoy choice food and sweet drinks" and share with others (v. 10).

As we see from reading Nehemiah 10–13, in the days and weeks that followed, the leaders were careful to fortify what God had done in the nation through the instituting and teaching of new laws. The revival continued to remind the people of Israel that Torah must be central to their lives.

Have the passages from Nehemiah and Psalm 119 softened your heart toward lawyers as well as law? If you still sense some hardness, realize that Paul was not just a missionary, preacher, and teacher, but also a "teacher of the Law" in ways similar to modern law professors and judges (see especially 1 Cor. 5–8, Galatians, and Romans). Do you love Jesus? Then you love the Man with the title, which can be Wonderful Counselor, Excellent Attorney, Extraordinary Strategist.

FAMOUS LAWYERS OF FAITH:

- John Calvin, the lawyer turned reformer
- Charles Finney, the lawyer turned evangelist who led the Second Great Awakening
- Abraham Lincoln, the lawyer turned president
- Hyman Appleman, the lawyer turned evangelist who inspired Billy Graham
- Pat Robertson, the lawyer turned televangelist
- Charles Colson, the lawyer turned convict turned founder of Prison Fellowship

With the knowledge of God's revealed love for Torah and for His children, dare we hope that He might use believers, godly lawyers, the Law, and even the reform of human law to more clearly reveal Himself and to bring about revival in the twenty-first century? In the coming chapters, we will consider ways any follower of Jesus can cooperate with the Holy Spirit in impacting the legal system.

Let us begin to see lawyers and their work as integral to the establishment of justice and mercy. We must possess a proper attitude toward attorneys so we can help those in the legal realm by:

1. evangelizing to the attorneys who have not trusted in Jesus;
2. encouraging believing attorneys who have yet to integrate their legal practice into Jesus' supervening call to make disciples and build His kingdom; and
3. engaging with those in the legal realm who are forcefully advancing God's kingdom.

"Justice Lifts the Nations,"
a 1904 mural by Paul Robert,
presides in the former Swiss
Supreme Court Building in
Lausanne, Switzerland. Justice
is personified by an imposing
lady dressed in radiant white.
In her right hand she lifts scales
signifying judicial fairness.
Her head is surrounded
by light suggesting divine
illumination. Twelve judges
surround her, looking up to her
for guidance. In her left hand
she holds a sword pointing to a
Bible, open and accessible to judges
and litigants alike. This artwork
encapsulates a message central
to Jesus in the Courtroom:
throughout the Bible, God
teaches true justice to judges,
lawyers, and all humanity.

Let us now consider how deeply involved many Christians in the legal system are in furthering the Great Commission. In carrying out that command of Jesus, our legal professionals have a special responsibility.

DOING JUSTICE, LOVING MERCY, WALKING HUMBLY

Whether judges, government lawyers, private-practice attorneys, legislators, or law professors, those in the legal system have always had the duty to "do justice and to love mercy and to walk humbly with [their] God" (Mic. 6:8). Those who have accepted the call to "walk humbly with God"—who are not the majority in most nations—have the particular privilege of helping politicians, other lawyers, and everyday citizens understand that all authority comes from God.

In 1961, five lawyers came together in Chicago to form the Christian Legal Society (CLS) to help Christian lawyers and law students integrate their faith into their legal practices through lawyer-directed discipleship, fellowship, religious liberty advocacy, and legal aid. CLS lawyers practice in all fields of law throughout the United States. And CLS partners with over fifty legal aid clinics across America that bring both the gospel and legal solutions to thousands every year. Yet CLS is not the only organization seeking to faithfully live out Micah 6:8. Here's another awesome legal organization that complements the work of CLS.

In 1994, realizing more could be done legally to protect and further religious freedom and the lives of unborn children, six Christian leaders, including Bill Bright (founder, Campus Crusade for Christ), Larry Burkett (chairman, Crown Financial Ministries), James Dobson (founder, Focus on the Family), D. James Kennedy (founder, Coral Ridge Ministries), Marlin Maddoux (president, International Christian Media), and

Donald Wildmon (founder, American Family Association), along with the leadership of over thirty other conservative Christian organizations, came together to found the Alliance Defense Fund, now known as the Alliance Defending Freedom (ADF). As the ADF website recounts:

> The morning Alliance Defending Freedom was launched, Dr. Bill Bright told a story about a little boy who was lost in a wheat field. The townspeople frantically searched for the boy, but they couldn't find him. Finally, one of the searchers suggested that they all hold hands and walk together across the field. They found the boy, but sadly, not in time to save his life. One of the searchers lamented, "If we had only linked arms sooner. . ."
>
> Dr. Bright compared the town's story to the Christian community.
>
> The gathered Christian leaders . . . recognized that Christians, like the town, needed to unite in order to defend religious freedom before it was too late.
>
> And so, Alliance Defending Freedom was launched on January 31, 1994, to ensure that religious freedom did not share the same fate as the boy in the field. . . .
>
> With that launch, the Christian community gained growing awareness that the threats to its freedom were multiplying. The legal system, which was built on a moral and Christian foundation, had been steadily moving against religious freedom, the sanctity of life, and marriage and family.[1]

By funding cases, training attorneys, and successfully advocating for equipping lawyers who focus on fighting for religious freedom in court, ADF challenged that movement. There are many other prominent organizations defending religious liberty. (See Appendix B; and links to all these ministries can be found at Jesusinthecourtroom.com.)

Likewise, many professors and leaders at Christian law schools have long known or have come to realize that "unless the LORD builds the house, the builders labor in vain" (Ps. 127:1). If legal training does not disciple and motivate the students to use their education to build God's kingdom, then what's the point? Many, if not most, law schools and law professors teach in a moral vacuum. Efforts to remedy that deficiency have turned to "ethics" as a possible remedy. However, the ethics propounded generally are founded on a human-centered worldview. Jesus spoke to world-centered values and behavior, stating, "For what profit is it to a man if he gains the whole world, and loses his own soul?" (Matt. 16:26 NKJV).

Our Wonderful Counselor is teaching us to restore God to the center of our thinking about our laws. Citizen-disciple, we must help these advocates. In so many ways they are our army on the front lines of spiritual warfare! Together, organizations like CLS and ADF—which are not ashamed of the name of Jesus—have won thousands of cases, discipled thousands of lawyers and law students, argued and won dozens of Supreme Court cases, initiated good laws, and defeated ungodly ones. Visit their websites, consult other believers, and pray until you sense which organization—or individual in an organization—aligns with your spiritual strengths that you can "adopt" for a month, a year, or other period of time. Support them however you can.

CITIZEN-DISCIPLE, WE MUST HELP THESE ADVOCATES. IN SO MANY WAYS THEY ARE OUR ARMY ON THE SPIRITUAL WARFARE FRONT LINES!

If you have children, grandchildren, nieces, nephews, or church members who are considering attending law school, first make sure they are introduced to Jesus as their Wonderful Counselor. Then support them spiritually and financially to attend where they can grow most in their faith. A list of faith-based and faith-friendly law schools is listed in Appendix B.

Most law schools, even the most secular, have already allowed, or would likely allow, a CLS law school chapter to be formed in conjunction with their institution. (The CLS website provides direction to those considering starting a chapter.) Of course, you can also recommend or give this book to potential law students or others who will be encouraged by it. *Redeeming Law: Christian Calling and the Legal Profession* by Michael P. Schutt is another excellent resource for law students and lawyers who follow Jesus and are seeking ways to better serve God in a legal vocation.

WAYS YOU CAN HELP BELIEVING LAWYERS AND LAW STUDENTS:

1. Give yourself a weekly calendar reminder for prayer
2. Get on at least one mailing list to know what to pray for
3. Support financially
4. Incorporate the insights and tools from Ephesians 6:11–18 into your battle plan

OBSTACLES LAWYERS FACE

If you want to help lawyers of faith, you should know some of the obstacles we face. Most are common to all believers but with a legal twist. I once had a dear client, a trucker whose company transported oversized boats, machinery, and other loads across the country. You've seen their parade going forty miles per hour on the interstate: a pace car with flashing dome light in front of a semi towing a behemoth generator on a flatbed followed by another car displaying the "OVERSIZED LOAD" sign larger than the car itself. Dave was a tough guy on the exterior, but he had an inner softness that seemed to grow ever gentler after he gave his life to Jesus in his mid-fifties.

As I provided legal counsel to Dave, I was privileged to offer him spiritual encouragement as well. I still remember his response to my advice for him to "let his light" shine to those customers, competitors, and highway officials who were making his life difficult. "John," he replied, "you don't know how difficult it is being a Christian in the trucking business. It's not like being a lawyer." I laughed and still remember his comment, because a few months later, another Christian client, a banker, said words to the same effect about the difficulty of identifying as a Jesus follower in the dirty world of banking—unlike in the dainty legal realm!

Jesus told us that if we live for Him we would lose family and friends, and be persecuted. He did not say it would be easier, or tougher, for truckers, bankers, or lawyers. I and my law partners, all of whom are believers, have lost clients, friends, or family because of our decision to follow Yeshua. Of course, we've gained the Friend who loves more deeply than a brother.

I recall the time one judge announced his decision against a church, Family Christian Fellowship, we represented. He was sputtering: "We're not going to have any ten-story prayer towers in Rockford!" (All we had sought was zoning approval to use for Sunday worship the gym of a vacant junior high the church had purchased.) No changes to the property were planned, much less the construction of a prayer tower. In fact, the trial contained no mention of the affiliation of the congregation with Oral Roberts University—which has a ten-story prayer tower—because we knew it should have been legally irrelevant. (Apparently the judge had engaged in improper extrajudicial fact-finding excursion about Family Christian Fellowship and Oral Roberts University.)

The Illinois Appellate Court, 2nd District, reversed the decision of the angry judge. About two hundred people were freed to worship the Lord in that space, though the church did suffer significant hardship and loss of members in the nine months it was prohibited from worship in its own building. The Appellate Court precedent has been cited many times in favor of allowing zoning relief to other churches. And get this: at the time of the litigation, a five-year-old boy in the Family Christian Fellowship congregation was learning to love Jesus. Oral Roberts Law School moved east to become a part of Regent University Law School. That little boy became a law student at Regent Law School and then a lawyer. Without either of us knowing the connection between Family Christian Fellowship and me, that young man, Noel Sterett, was hired by Mauck & Baker in 2006 and is now a partner! You will read about a case he won for the Lord in the next chapter, in the section "A Miracle in Sauk City."

Jesus' teaching about the duty, cost, and blessing of being His disciple applies to everyone, no matter what one's occupation is. Yet Christian lawyers and lawmakers, by virtue of their work, have a larger-than-average circle of influence.

ONE BELIEVER'S PATH TO SERVING GOD IN LAW

Here's a story of another man's journey to serving God as a lawyer:

> My name is Sorin A. Leahu and I am an attorney with the law firm of Mauck & Baker, LLC in Chicago. I was born in a much different time and place. My story begins in Arad, a city in Romania located near the Hungarian border. The year

was 1988, and Romania was entering its forty-first year under Communist rule. Like all countries under Communism, widespread poverty and suffering were the norm. Moreover, civil rights violations and religious persecutions were extensive.

When Communism ended in 1989, travel slowly opened up for those seeking a better life. Obtaining visas and travel documents, however, was a difficult task. In 1990, the US developed a lottery system that granted visas to a limited number of lucky winners. The lottery system is still used today, but the odds of winning are still remarkably low. In 2010, for example, 15 million people worldwide applied for visas through the lottery but only 50,000, one in 300, were granted. My family applied for visas through this same system, hoping and praying for a miracle. In 1995, we learned that our names had been selected in the lottery.

Upon arriving in Chicago, my parents emphasized two qualities: hard work and education. Because my parents valued education, they were set on sending my brother and me to a school near our home. This school was rated among the best in the state and therefore difficult to get into. In fact, the only way to be admitted was through another lottery system. My parents submitted applications, hoping and praying that they would win a lottery yet again. God responded, and both my brother and I were admitted into the school. This particular school proved pivotal in my upbringing and instilled in me a love for learning that ultimately led me to college and law school.

Although God's hand was in all of this, I did not see it at the time. It took a couple more years, shortly before high school, before I decided to make a personal decision to follow Christ. Making that decision started me on my spiritual walk, and I began thinking about what God wanted for my life.

Entering college, law school was not on my radar. I was still praying for wisdom and direction as I waited for a clear answer. At that time, I worked as an insurance agent at an agency close to campus. I was studying business, was fully licensed, and planned on having a successful career in the insurance industry. In my junior year, I was required to take a course in business law. The professor assigned to teach this course happened to be a Christian attorney allied with the Alliance Defending Freedom (ADF), a Christian legal organization. My relationship with this professor developed into one of discipleship, and I slowly began to explore law. Perhaps it should come as no surprise that the area of law that most stirred me was religious liberty work. Coming from a background where civil rights and religious liberties had been denied to people for over forty years, I felt a passion and a calling to join the fight.

This passion kept me focused during the trials of law school. It further motivated me to participate in a program called the Blackstone Legal Fellowship. The Fellowship is a nine-week program for Christian law students organized by ADF. This program provided me the foundation upon which to build the rest of my career. It also introduced me to the firm of Mauck & Baker, LLC, where I served as a summer intern. Again, God was placing me in the right places at the right times with the right people, guiding me toward my calling.

As He had done in the past, God continued to intervene in my life after law school. Although I had hoped to work in the area of religious liberty following graduation, positions for this type of work were not available at the time. Mauck & Baker would have been ideal, but they were not hiring, either.

Instead, I took a job doing insurance defense work. I had no interest in this type of work and felt quite disappointed that I was not doing what I felt I should be doing. Through those low moments, God taught me to lean on Him, to wait, and to trust Him. Only after I learned these lessons did God make His move.

I was praying on my way to work one morning, talking to God about my circumstances and next steps in life. After I finished praying, I received a text from one of the partners at Mauck & Baker. One of their associates was leaving, and the firm wondered whether I would consider joining them— with no lottery even required! As in other critical moments in my life, prayer opened doors that seemed firmly shut. It was incredible to see God work in such a real way and in direct response to prayer and trust. Because of this, I now have the privilege of working on behalf of churches and ministries across the country ensuring that their doors remain open to continue doing what God has called them to do.

RELEASING CAPTIVES

Innocent people are sometimes wrongly convicted. If you are ever arrested, one of your first thoughts probably will be, "Where can I find a good lawyer?" Jesus cares, and wants us to care, about those who are behind bars. Our Wonderful Counselor tells us He has come "to proclaim freedom for the prisoners" (Luke 4:18). I believe this promise from Jesus is both metaphorical (to captives of sin), but also literal (to those in prison). One example of how these words of the Messiah are being fulfilled is through the improvement in the Australian justice system by an attorney who was touched by God.

Bob Moles, affiliated with Advocates International (see sidebar for information), shares in his own words how our Wonderful Counselor saved him and then called him to serve as a lawyer:

> As a postgraduate student, I was studying philosophy (especially the works of David Hume and Immanuel Kant) at Edinburgh University to try to prove that Christians were deluded. A friend then advised me to read the works of Thomas Aquinas. I had no intention of doing so. The following week, my PhD supervisor, a world-leading legal theorist, apologized to me for spending the remaining money in the faculty library budget so foolishly—the sum of money he had matched exactly the reduced price of a full set of the *Summa Theologiae* (Aquinas' *magnum opus*) from the local bookshop. So he bought it. He knew that I would not have approved. I felt obliged to read the first volume. When I did, I was able to see with perfect clarity that the delusions had been all mine.

I had worked in Belfast throughout the years of violence from the Irish Republican Army which brought home to me the importance of the rule of law. Many years later, when I arrived in South Australia to teach law, some students pointed out to me a possible miscarriage of justice case. I soon realized that there had in fact been a very serious systemic error that had given rise to a great many innocent people being held in prison. After the airing of our first national television program, I was told by the dean of the law school where I was teaching that my research on this topic was "contentious" and would not be consistent with my job as a law professor. I was obliged to give up my academic employment in order to do what I knew God had asked me to do. Of that there could be no doubt. My previous experiences had now gifted me with the insight into a devastating legal and social problem. My experiences had also given me the skills to be able to do something about it. And most convincingly, there was nobody else ready or willing to take it on.

I now know that God had been training me all this time without my knowing it. My experiences, my intellectual knowledge, the seemingly random job opportunities all were part of His plan—to set the innocent prisoners free. And the most glorious thing of all was that He had invited me to tackle this important work for Him.

Advocates like Bob Moles and Bibi Sangha are part of a global network of legal professionals who are following Jesus and changing the legal systems of nations. Advocates International is that ministry.

Founded in 1991 by the second executive director of the Christian Legal Society, Sam Ericsson, their mission is to encourage, empower, and equip attorneys worldwide to meet locally, organize nationally, cooperate regionally, and link globally to promote religious freedom, justice for the poor, rule of law, human life and dignity, peace and reconciliation, family and community, and ethical integrity. Find their website in Appendix B.

Over the last sixteen years, Christian attorney Bob Moles and his wife, Bibi Sangha, established and developed the Networked Knowledge research program to deal with serious miscarriages of justice in Australia. One focus of the program is to ensure that defective cases were reviewed by the courts. They soon found there was a problem. In Australia, once a person had been convicted and had lost an appeal, afterwards, if subsequent evidence showed they were innocent, they did not have any further right of appeal. Moles and Bibi persuaded the Human Rights Commission of Australia that this was contrary to Australia's international human rights obligations. This led to legislative change in South Australia and Tasmania—the only substantive changes to the criminal appeal rights in Australia in over a hundred years. As a result of those changes, cases are now being reviewed by the appeal court. Here are some examples:

- Henry Keogh, imprisoned for over twenty years for the murder of his fiancée. His conviction was overturned by the court in 2014. It was accepted that the "mechanism of murder" was "mere speculation" and had no scientific support.

- Frits Van Beelen, imprisoned for over seventeen years for the murder of a young girl. An appeal court has accepted that the forensic evidence as to time of death had no scientific support. It is now the subject of appeal to Australia's highest court.

- Derek Bromley, still in prison after thirty-three years for murder and ten years over his non-parole period. The case against him is now shown to be fundamentally flawed and awaits determination by the appeal court.

He cannot apply for parole because he refuses to say he is sorry, which would be an admission of guilt.

Godly laws recognize the limitations in human nature and ultimately the limitations in our human-made legal systems to obtain absolute certainty. Deuteronomy 19:15 states, "One witness is not enough to convict anyone accused of any crime or offense they may have committed. A matter must be established by the testimony of two or three witnesses." While such a godly legal mandate implicitly allows guilty people to be acquitted on the "technicality" of only one witness, it ultimately wants us to prioritize the protection of innocent people from false conviction.

Advocates International is up against many powerful and well-funded opponents. Bob and his team are, as he puts it, "just a few unfunded individual lawyers seeking to find and uphold the truth." They face much opposition from those in positions of ostensible authority within the local community. In addition, the law being the law, cases can drag on for months or even years.

But God's people have stepped up to support the work of freeing the innocent. Bob shares:

> In that context [of long, drawn-out cases and opposition] it becomes important to have the reassurance, love, and commitment from local people who understand the difficulties but who can also generate the spiritual firepower to recharge the batteries through long months and sometimes years of obfuscation and delay. When we attended a parliamentary inquiry, the room was full to overflowing with prayerful supporters who transformed the atmosphere within the room. It led to the first major change to the appeal rights anywhere in Australia in

over a hundred years. That subsequently gave Henry Keogh his freedom after twenty years imprisonment. It has given hope to countless others.

To know that we have eyes and prayers supporting this cause from overseas and within the local community sends a powerful message to those who would usurp judicial authority and encourages those most in need of it.

God has time and again used renewed focus on His Law to bring revival and has raised up thousands of lawyers in the United States and around the world to protect and advance legal freedom so God's love could be made known.

Now, come with me to see how a group of three inner-city Chicago churches full of non-lawyers, empowered by our Wonderful Counselor through the Holy Spirit, engaged the legal system and fought for justice and mercy.

CHAPTER 3

LEGAL ADVANCES THROUGH WONDERFUL COUNSELOR JESUS

In the Sermon on the Mount, Jesus proclaims the blessedness of those who, in our English translations, are variously called "poor in spirit" or "the meek." He was referencing a Hebrew concept and word as He taught from Psalm 37:11: "But the meek [*anavim*] will inherit the land and enjoy great peace." I like to call them "the little people," because it describes a society where politicians, celebrities, and lawyers are considered the "big people." Many, often due to their "bigness," miss the blessing and spiritual effectiveness that God reserves for the humble. All throughout Scripture, we find instances of "little people" doing mighty acts for God. No matter who you are—whether you are a lawyer or a non-lawyer—you can impact the legal system for God's glory and the advancement of His kingdom. Join me as we visit two extraordinary moves of our Wonderful Counselor, the Extraordinary Strategist, through humble people: one through prayer, legislation, and litigation; the second through prayer at the courthouses of America.

THE PRAYERS OF THE *ANAVIM*

It was still light on that beautiful June day in 2000 in Chicago's blue-collar Portage Park neighborhood. The Iglesia Monte de Sion Wednesday evening prayer meeting had started to roll. Two synthesizers were rattling the stained glass in the simple, 1920s-era brick church building. The building looked like it had been recycled from German Lutheran immigrants, and it was surrounded by rundown bungalows and walk-up apartments. The shouted prayers energized by a raucous praise band had quickly gripped my heart, and I could have easily let the tears cascade. Who did they think they were? What raw faith was I feeling? An inner-city congregation of illegal Mexican immigrants and other working-class Hispanics—many, if not most, "undocumented"—approached the God of heaven, asking Him to plant dynamite sticks, as it were, under a legislative logjam 700 miles to the east in the United States Congress.

Pastor Jose Acevedo had just introduced me to the hundred or so church members assembled to talk—well, shout—to God. Since the music team and worship leader had already elevated our praise, three questions raced through my mind:

1. As I led prayer during a portion of the service, would I raise my voice and pace to maintain the fervency of the congregation, or would I "be myself" and sober them to my accustomed Presbyterian "decent and in order" prayer style?

2. Was I, a lawyer educated at two of America's finest universities, willing to humble myself to receive prayer and ministry from uneducated dishwashers, homemakers, and gardeners?

3. Would I believe that these followers of Jesus, most of whom could not even speak English, could understand the nuances of zoning and land use law and fathom the workings of Congress, much less pray effectively?

And a fourth question preceded the others: how did I get here? After two Supreme Court decisions in the 1990s limiting religious freedom, lawyers and leaders of faith groups gathered together in the fall of 1997 to begin the process of drafting a new law to neutralize, or at least lessen, the effect of those decisions. With my years of experience in real estate and church zoning litigation, I was invited to participate on a large conference call. I suggested the new law should include a land use section requiring equal zoning treatment for churches and religious assemblies, when compared to nonreligious "assembly" uses, and that every municipal zoning code must include an area where religious assemblies were freely permitted. Doug Laycock, then Professor of Law at the University of Texas, drafted the bill then called the Religious Liberty Protection Act. He added an important third prong to the land use section: if the zoning "substantially burdened" the religious assembly, the municipality must prove it had a "compelling governmental interest" narrowly tailored to achieve that purpose.

In March 1998, I testified before the Subcommittee on the Constitution of the House Judiciary Committee, sharing examples of religious land use problems including new churches being effectively zoned out of most areas of Chicago and aldermanic antagonism and abuse when exceptions to the harsh rules were requested. "These laws can be abused . . . in approximately half of all city ordinances that I have read . . .

[there are no zones] where a church can freely go," I testified.

After the hearings in 1998, the bill went up for a vote in the House the following summer. A 306–118 vote put the Religious Liberty Protection Act into the committee system before it could be voted on by the Senate. Although the complicated system can provide thoroughness, it is an alligator pond where fledgling legislation can be quietly chomped (amended) to death. The opposition from both gay-rights groups and municipalities supported by Senator Daniel Moynihan of New York appeared formidable as the Religious Liberty Protection Act was apparently too risky for many politicians to support publicly. Nothing happened.

Then in early 2000 after four years of logjam, the chairman of Civil Liberties for Urban Believers (C.L.U.B.), Theodore Wilkinson, organized prayer meetings in three inner-city Chicago churches to intercede for the bill to move out of the Senate. On the third Wednesdays of April, May, and June 2000, Christians in Chicago came together and prayed. Those meetings were amazing because there were no other lawyers in attendance. Those who gathered may not have been experts in law, but they prayed with fervent determination to God to pass the federal legislation protecting the religious freedom of believers to acquire property for worship.

A MIRACLE IN WASHINGTON, D.C.

While the bill was buried in the Senate during 1999 and early 2000, my participation in seeing the bill pass ceased other than a periodic phone call to my contacts at the Christian Legal Society who would with discouragement report "no progress." But after reading an op-ed opposing the Religious Land Use and Institutionalized Persons Act in the July 27, 2000, issue of

The New York Times, I called Carl Esbeck and Sam Casey at the Christian Legal Society to see what triggered the article.

They were ecstatic, telling me a "miracle" had happened: the bill providing religious groups the right to land use protection had finally passed! The Religious Liberty Protection Act had been renamed the Religious Land Use and Institutionalized Persons Act (RLUIPA) to reduce the scope to include only religious land use and prisoner rights. Prominent Senators from both political parties began to lobby for RLUIPA— both eliminating opposition and gaining support for the bill. Edward Kennedy, one of the most liberal members of the Senate, and Orrin Hatch, one of the most conservative members of the Senate, were the two major sponsors of the bill, making it a bipartisan effort. Because of the narrowed focus, the gay-rights lobby dropped its opposition. Senator Daniel Patrick Moynihan, who had been one of the leading opponents of RLUIPA, "inexplicably" dropped his opposition. President Clinton also signaled his support of the bill. But the municipalities, not wanting to relinquish a speck of control, and *The New York Times* remained strongly opposed.

The Christian Legal Society attorneys reported that one of the Senate sponsors had presented a routine procedural motion to the full Senate in July, believing it would, if approved, send the bill to a joint House-Senate committee for further hearings—which meant more dangers and more delays. Thus, it received unanimous Senate approval as one of the final pieces of business on the last day before the summer adjournment of Congress. As the Senate was closing down, news arrived from the House of Representatives that the House adjournment had been unexpectedly delayed for procedural reasons. Sam Casey, president of the Christian Legal Society, took the paperwork from the just-approved Senate motion and ran it over to Representative Charles Canady of Florida, one of the House sponsors of the bill, for possible action.

The municipal opposition could and probably should have had a House member stand by to object to any maneuver to slip the law through by a unanimous vote. If only one House member objected to unanimous passage, the bill would go back into the committee labyrinth. This is essentially what happened next:

Rep. Canady: "Mr. Speaker, the Senate has just passed Bill S.2869 unanimously. I now move for unanimous approval by the House."

Speaker of the House: "Is there any opposition?"

[Pause]

"Hearing none."

[Gavel resounds]

"Senate Bill 2869 is approved unanimously."

After four years of delay, within a single hour RLUIPA had, despite serious opposition, been sent to the president by unanimous approval in both branches of Congress! The approval came almost one month to the day after the three prayer meetings and the same day *The New York Times* editorialized against it—Thursday, July 27, 2000. Two months later, President Clinton signed RLUIPA into law.

How does RLUIPA work?

As the Supreme Court has long interpreted the Constitution, the states and municipalities are the primary authorities over zoning and other land-use regulations. That authority has always been tempered by the US Constitution's protection of private property. States can regulate, but they cannot confiscate, and the regulations cannot be arbitrary. Until the 1980s, the states had broad leeway in the zoning of churches. As I read the cases at the time—and I'm generalizing—if a church in the West or Northeast needed a zoning change to build or relocate, it was usually denied. Churches in the Midwest had a fair chance of obtaining a zoning permit, and churches in the South received good treatment. But ominous legal trends were developing:

1. Zoning everywhere was becoming more restrictive. About every ten to fifteen years, municipalities would revise their codes comprehensively. I've never seen a code anywhere that was simpler than the one it replaced. Specialists called "land planners" arose, creating increased regulations and making a living showing developers and other land users how to comply.

2. Voters, homeowners in particular, in complicity with municipal authorities had figured out how to turn zoning from shield into selfishness. Zoning codes can reasonably be used to prevent a gas station being built in a residential neighborhood because it could be a nuisance to residents and cause the property value of homeowners to decline. However, the codes were increasingly used for such purposes as prohibiting development of a forty-acre tract for forty homes even though the tract was surrounded by homes on one-acre parcels! The professed reason for disallowing a new development with identical density to the surrounding existing development would often be to prevent "overcrowding," but a strong underlying motive was for homeowners who elected the "judges" (a.k.a., the city council and zoning board) to improve their own home values at the expense of the hapless farmer who had grown corn until he retired instead of selling his forty acres earlier. In other words,

zoning boards and homeowners would reduce, without compensation, the property rights of another to enrich the homeowners.

3. America got wheels. In the 1920s to 1950s, when zoning was coming into vogue, most churchgoers would attend a congregation near their homes, usually in their own town. A practical result of local attendance was that city councils could be held accountable by church members as voters. An increasingly automobiled society—sometimes eight to twelve wheels per household—arrived in the 1950s and is with us still today. Most church attendees tell me they drive past five or ten other churches to reach the one they prefer due to tradition, preaching, worship style, family connections, and other reasons. Proximity is rarely the deciding factor in church attendance these days. Unfortunately, this growing remoteness weakened political accountability. During church requests for "Special Use" permits, I've heard zoning boards ask the legally irrelevant question, "How many of your members live in this town?"

4. America secularized. The number of people regularly attending services has dropped. Besides having less political influence over zoning decisions—which should be nonpolitical—the result of fewer churchgoers has led to a decreased understanding of the value of a church to a community. Council members and zoning boards generally are a cross-section of the citizenry. Where there are fewer believers, or the believers are not citizen-disciples, there are fewer municipal authorities who understand how churches build up people and thereby strengthen communities.

I've seen the problem close up in Chicago with inner-city storefront churches. And yet, the inner-city church is often the only organization serving people in the community, from the bottom up, in ways such as:

- helping young people stay out of jail;
- encouraging marriage;
- giving the lonely and elderly a place to belong;
- pooling resources or sharing apartments or homes when members face eviction or foreclosure; and
- giving members life training in service and leadership.

How well has human-centered law, what I would call a "govern and supply from the top down and marginalize God" legal system, done in:

- providing security from violence;
- fostering fatherhood and stable families;
- reducing drug use;
- eliminating gangs;
- educating young people; and
- creating jobs?

With churches being the primary providers of ministry to the people, why do cities so often use zoning to make locating or expanding a church in the inner-city (and suburbs) so difficult? When we look closely, we see the problem is too much government land regulation. But can we also see how God, in response to prayer, turned what is sometimes injustice but is often persecution into blessings through RLUIPA. Rejoice with one of probably thousands of accounts of how RLUIPA has allowed the gospel to go forward.

A MIRACLE IN SAUK CITY

Do you believe in miracles? Put another way, do you believe God can produce otherwise inexplicable results through men and women—be they lawyers or judges, real estate closers, bankers, or pastors? The congregation of River Hills Community Church in Sauk City, Wisconsin, certainly does.

The River Hills congregation, founded in 2005, had struggled and prayed like so many other small churches in America to find a place to call their own—moving from one inadequate leased space to another. After a five-year search, the congregation finally found in late 2013 a building that fit their needs and wouldn't break the bank. In fact, the building was a bank, and the bank was even willing to finance the purchase.

This was an answer to their prayers. Pastor Dennis Virta had been teaching his congregation that God's will and ways are not always the path of least resistance. In fact, it seldom is. They had persevered in prayer, received an answer, and were ready to move—or so they thought. As God would have it, however, there was more work to be done in their hearts, in the hearts of others in the community, and in the legal system. After River Hills had the property under contract, they quickly found themselves up against a hostile zoning official and a zoning code that discriminated against religious assemblies. Contrary to RLUIPA, Sauk City's zoning code did not permit, absent explicit city authorization, any new churches to locate anywhere in the community. Yet Sauk City freely allowed nonreligious assemblies like community centers and libraries to operate at the property River Hills hoped to buy. But how many churches knew about RLUIPA?

Faced with this unwarranted hostility and unjust zoning code, the church knew that it simply could not afford to proceed with the purchase without zoning approval. To make matters worse, once the bank learned of Sauk City's opposition to the church's location, it withdrew its offer to finance the purchase, leaving the church with little more than a week not only to come up with nearly $300,000 to purchase the property, but also overcome Sauk City's zoning opposition.

Without faith, all of this new resistance did not look like a providential opportunity, but rather like an opportunity for further unbelief, discouragement, and resentment. Thankfully, Pastor Virta was able to connect to the attorneys at Mauck & Baker. Together we immediately set about the gospel work of righting the wrongs, exposing the injustice, filing for legal protection, and trusting in the Lord. With just a few days to go before the church had to close on the property or lose it, we filed a federal lawsuit on January 28, 2014, against Sauk City, requesting an emergency order requiring the city to allow River Hills to use the property for religious assembly as RLUIPA required. Over the next three days, we negotiated with Sauk City's attorney to see if the village would agree to an order allowing the church in. Meanwhile, Pastor Virta and his congregation set about praying as they scrambled to raise the money needed by week's end to close the deal. On the eve of the closing date, the church had neither the funds nor Sauk City's agreement. An emergency hearing was scheduled in court, and the closing was still scheduled to take place at the title company. How would God pull this off?

On the morning of the next day, January 31, 2014, and just three days after filing a federal lawsuit, Sauk City relented and agreed to drop its zoning opposition. United States District Judge William Conley then entered an order allowing River Hills Community Church to move in. The prospect of facing a large claim for damages may have helped persuade the city. Backed by RLUIPA, this church was able to keep its hope alive but still had to come up with the money.

Buoyed by the court order, Pastor Virta and the members of the congregation increased the fervency of their prayers and began giving like never before. Members began pulling from their savings and retirement accounts. People began to wire money from all over to try to close the deal before the wire transfer line at the title company's bank closed at three o'clock on Friday afternoon. At 2:19 that afternoon, Pastor Virta emailed the congregation,

> We are down to the wire, trusting God that the necessary loaned funds will be on deposit by 2:45 for a 3 p.m. closing on River Hills first building! . . . This is an amazing ride. Let's remember Psalm 127:1:
> "Unless the LORD builds the house, the builders labor in vain. Unless the LORD watches over the city, the guards stand watch in vain."
> I have had the privilege of watching God make this whole thing happen when, it seemed, everyone in the real estate world said it wouldn't happen. One Village official said repeatedly "THIS IS A DEAD ISSUE!" Well, GOD IS IN THE RESURRECTION BUSINESS! What was dead is now alive, and all glory goes to God!! The Lord IS building this house, and there isn't a question in my mind. I'll keep you posted.

Over the next twenty minutes, Pastor Virta, the church's attorney, the closer, the realtor, and even the director of the chamber of commerce watched God work. In utter jubilation, Pastor Virta wrote a follow-up email in which he reported:

> I just received word that we are over the top! WAY over the top on the money necessary to close 30 minutes from now.

At noon our closing attorney was worried. Now he is amazed. That's God! That's the Church! That's the Holy Spirit! That's River Hills! . . . God and our church rose to the occasion to make our own bridge loan to make this happen. God brought us right to the raw edge of faith . . . then catapulted us across!! . . . Thank you for being used of God to help make this all happen. More work yet to be done. Much more. The realtor is in awe. The Chamber of Commerce director is crying with joy and amazement (she and family attend once in a while). The attorney is shaking his head saying he has never seen any deal like this.

RLUIPA'S NATIONAL IMPACT

Computer searches in legal databases show that since July 27, 2000, 500 or more land-use cases have been decided by enforcing, construing, or referencing the provisions of RLUIPA. (There are also many thousands of cases where prisoners obtained greater religious freedom through RLUIPA protection while incarcerated.) For every actual court decision, experience tells us about ten RLUIPA land-use cases are settled or approved administratively. Beyond that are the hundreds of towns, villages, and cities that, in the spirit of obeying the law, have amended their ordinances to conform with federal law by:

1. removing onerous zoning restrictions on new church buildings;
2. allowing conversions of manufacturing buildings, warehouses, and surplus schools into houses of worship;
3. facilitating approval of religious communes, homeless shelters, half-way houses, and other faith-based ministries;

4. changing their zoning maps to enlarge areas where such uses have been allowed;

5. reforming zoning laws that impose one-size-fits-all categories for religious assemblies, regardless of size.

Certainly, many decisions have been made against people of faith, and many battles remain. However, I believe these victories are the result of the prayers of 300 to 400 people in Chicago back in 2000 and of the efforts and prayers of many others, over many years, appealing to the Wonderful Counselor and using the weapons of their warfare (see 2 Cor. 10:4). Of course, this particular battle for religious freedom is not really about buildings, court rulings, or abstract legal principles. Yeshua, our amazing advocate, gave His life for His people. The tens of thousands of congregations enabled to flourish by enactment and enforcement of RLUIPA have certainly brought the gospel message, love of God's people, and discipleship to millions who otherwise would have been kept from hearing the Word or connecting to believers.

So, citizen-disciple, do not be discouraged when you encounter legal obstacles to living out your faith or when someone says, "What can you do? You're just a little person." Our God is able! Two Scriptures come to mind:

> When the enemy shall come in like a flood, the Spirit of the Lord shall lift up a standard against him. (Isa. 59:19b kjv)

> About midnight Paul and Silas were praying and singing hymns to God, and the other prisoners were listening to them. Suddenly there was such a violent earthquake that the foundations of the prison were shaken. At once all the prison doors flew open, and everyone's chains came loose. (Acts 16:25–26)

A DAD, HIS KIDS, AND THE LAW

One dad we know talks frequently about legal issues with his three school-age children. He said, "Once we started focusing on legal things, it turned into table conversation. Our three children understand some of the battles we face—bakers, florists, T-shirt makers, pharmacies, and Christian foster agencies shut down because they believe their actions cooperating with the gay/lesbian agenda will cause some to feel their homosexual conduct, including the rampant promiscuity often involved, is sanctioned or approved by believers. We talk about elections, political candidates, character, how to make ethical decisions, court cases, and judges. We support ADF and Administer Justice (an organization that provides legal help for the poor). And in the future? One might be a teacher, one a counselor or doctor, and one, who needs a battle to fight, I could see becoming a lawyer. I would offer extra encouragement if any of them felt called to law. There is a dearth of sold-out Christian lawyers!"

So what happened at the Portage Park prayer meeting? It continued as it started—full of fervency. We also prayed fervently at Christ Center International, a predominantly African American congregation (in a converted funeral home) on Chicago's south side and at His Word to All Nations, a predominantly blue-collar white congregation on the southwest side of the city. These C.L.U.B. churches, through prayer, experienced a huge legal breakthrough for the kingdom. God blessed congregations across America by also using lawyers such as Carl Esbeck, Sam Casey, and Doug Laycock, as well as the prayer efforts of many others. Now learn of and enjoy the taste of thousands of prayer victories in an ongoing move of God that is spreading to litigants, criminals, jurors, lawyers, and judges at courthouses across America.

HOW THE MEEK IMPACT THE WORLD

Encouraged? The examples of believers cooperating with each other and using Holy Spirit gifts and legal gifts in coordination can give us renewed determination, knowing we don't need to be a Supreme Court justice or the president to impact our nation's legal system for God's kingdom.

Why did God use the meek, the *anavim*, to pray through major legislation? Why did God use a log cabin–born lawyer to bring Emancipation? Why was the Savior born in a stable? Why did God use little Israel instead of Egypt, Babylon, Greece, or Rome to reveal Himself to humanity? Why is God calling you, who are probably not a lawyer or bigwig,[1] to impact our legal system for His kingdom? To help us answer this important question, let me introduce you to a person and a ministry assisting followers of Jesus to impact the legal realm worldwide.

THE EXAMPLES OF BELIEVERS COOPERATING WITH EACH OTHER AND USING HOLY SPIRIT GIFTS AND LEGAL GIFTS IN COORDINATION CAN GIVE US RENEWED DETERMINATION, KNOWING WE DON'T NEED TO BE A SUPREME COURT JUSTICE OR THE PRESIDENT TO IMPACT OUR NATION'S LEGAL SYSTEM FOR GOD'S KINGDOM.

Tyler Makepeace is one of the humblest lawyers I have ever met. At age fifty-five, twice divorced, and, in his words, "going down for the third time," this family law practitioner met the Man from Nazareth. He started life anew, forgiven and with a much softened heart for those experiencing divorce and other legal traumas. So changed was Tyler that he began to pray for and with litigants, lawyers, court personnel, and judges during his frequent trips to the county courthouse in Colorado Springs. So receptive to prayer were those he prayed with that he and other believers set up a table on public property near the courthouse entrance and hung across it a banner reading "Need Prayer?" It's a simple model that has yielded profound results. They called it "Court-side Ministries."

Many pastors have told me that their favorite ministry times are not Sunday morning services, but rather funerals and weddings, because when someone has died or two people wed, the congregation is more likely to be full of backsliders, nonbelievers, seekers, and reexaminers of the faith—who often sob with regret or cry with joy. The fishing is good when hearts are soft. Do you know, or are you, a pastor or evangelist who has fished diligently but has caught little in the past few months or years? Well, Jesus has a word for you to receive or relay to discouraged fishers of men: "'Throw your net on the right side of the boat and you will find some.' When they did, they were unable to haul the net in because of the large number of fish" (John 21:6).

Between eight and eleven o'clock in the morning most weekdays and at countless courthouses across the world, the fish are ready. Who are they?

Tamara, a desperate mother who, like Tyler Makepeace, is facing her third divorce. Due to her drinking problem, she faces the loss of custody of her beloved six-year-old daughter. Her husband is not only seeking divorce, but also wants to drastically restrict the amount of time that Tamara can visit her daughter. In turn, her daughter also faces loss: the presence of her mother.

Alex and Jill, a childless couple in their late thirties. Full of joy and thanksgiving, they have arrived to complete the adoption of a special-needs infant who has fulfilled their long-frustrated hope to become parents. Sadly, they know not whom to thank or how to express the gratitude stirring deeply in their souls.

A quavering twenty-three-year-old first-time juror. Sandra

Jane is returning to vote in the death penalty phase for a homeless man who stabbed to death another homeless man to steal $50.

An embittered fifty-year-old businessman. Mr. Lewinski harbors a dream of vengeance toward a former friend who accidentally slammed a cab door on his hand, leading to the amputation of four fingers. His lawyer is pressing him to settle for the $50,000 insurance limit because the friend has few assets, but Mr. Lewinski wants blood.

Who else? Brothers at odds over an inheritance. An elderly couple seeking a thirty-day extension before the sheriff puts their meager belongings on the street. Thousands upon thousands are the poignant stories, the pregnant opportunities for Jesus to minister to those with open and seeking hearts.

Do you think any of these people would welcome prayer and be open to the gospel message, to repentance, to forgiveness, to referral to a Bible-teaching church, or to Christian counseling? If you answered "yes," I suspect you may have John 4:35 in your heart: "Don't you have a saying, 'It's still four months until harvest'? I tell you, open your eyes and look at the fields! They are ripe for harvest."

PHOTO COURTESY OF COURTSIDE MINISTRIES

Tyler Makepeace

PHOTO COURTESY OF COURTSIDE MINISTRIES

Prayer at the Courthouse

Thomas Strening, one of the leaders at Courtside Ministries, told me two of his favorite testimonies. The first is of a man who had been released from prison early one morning, around five o'clock to be exact. He was still waiting to be picked up by his mother when Courtside arrived. His story was typical. He had done wrong but did not have money for bail, and so he sat in prison. He stole a hat at Walmart. He had several priors (previous offenses), so the judge would not let him out without bail. Weeks went by. The judge went on vacation, the prosecutor went out of town, and his public defender was not available some weeks because of travel. Finally, after almost seven weeks, he appeared before the judge who released him since he had already served so much time. In the early morning hours, he slept by a garbage can for his shelter as he waited for his ride. Strening looked at him and did something he said he almost never does. He confronted the man's unbelief directly and firmly. He asked him, "If Christ loved you so much that He died for you, why would you steal a hat? If you need one, just ask Him for one!"

The man lit up, not in anger, but with excitement. "Look," he said. "Do you see this hat I have? I found it on top of the garbage can I was sleeping by this morning. It's a fitted cap! It's monogrammed and fits perfectly! They must not want it since they left it with the trash!"

Strening replied, "Glad you understand, my friend. He loves you and will take care of you."

The second story begins one morning at 26th and California—the Chicago criminal court—where a young woman was struggling to walk down the stairs exiting the courthouse. She was actually walking sideways because of an infection in her leg bone. If that infection got into her hip, her hip bone might have to be replaced. It hurt Strening to see her in so much pain, and he asked her if he could pray with her. She said yes. He commanded the pain to leave her in Jesus' name, and they prayed for about two minutes. He asked her how she was feeling, and she asked, "What just happened to me? I'm not hurting anymore!"

He told her Jesus just kissed her. She kept remarking about how this was so astonishing to her. Strening then asked, "Would you like Him to do for your heart what He just did for your leg?"

"Yes," she said. "I am ready!" She prayed to commit her life to Christ in front of those same steps she had so much trouble with before.

Here's another testimony from a recent Courtside Ministries newsletter:

> A group of three women, all mothers, spontaneously converged at our table. To their surprise and ours, each one of them had lost a son that was murdered. We perceived this as a holy moment. We asked our infinitely loving God to minister to them and He, in His faithfulness, showed up and ministered deeply to them. Two mothers extended forgiveness to the perpetrator; one went deeper in her commitment with Jesus. They embraced one another after the prayer, and spoke words of comfort, understanding each other's pain. One mother wept as she shared that her son had been murdered in the previous forty-eight hours. Our volunteers embraced them, and gave a couple of referrals to faith-based counseling.

The testimonies are not limited to those who receive prayer; blessings flow back to those who pray. I asked my nephew Derek Boundy, who has been a Courtside volunteer at the Lake County Courthouse in Waukegan, Illinois, for about a year, to describe how his weekly prayer time there has helped him to participate in the work of our Wonderful Counselor and Savior Jesus. He wrote:

> After twenty-plus years as a believer, I can truly say I have never been on fire as much as I am now. This is a direct result of serving our Lord at Courtside Ministries. As I prayed about what to say in regard to my experience with Courtside, the Lord told me He came for the sick and not the well. We serve the lost, the hurting, the non-churchgoers, the atheists, the agnostics, and every single person from the homeless to the billionaire.
>
> Each of my three children—ages fifteen, thirteen, and ten— has on occasion served, prayed, and ministered with me at Courtside. There is nothing quite like hearing a child pray for someone. This is especially fun when those we pray with have a look of awe on their face at how touched they are by the Lord from the mouths of babes. My ten-year-old son has gone with me many times. He has prayed for many and has seen mighty works of the Holy Spirit.
>
> The vast majority of my spiritual laziness has disappeared, thanks to the countless blessings and opportunities provided by our Lord at Courtside. There is a constant inflow of "sick," who recognize the soul cancer that we all suffer from. They are swimming in a contaminated river, gasping for anything or anyone to help them find clean water. They are going in and out of local county courthouses daily. We have the wonderful opportunity to lead them to that eternal flow of living water that forever refreshes and renews.
>
> The workers are few that will help them exit the dirty river and enter the pure river of eternal life of which they will never thirst or hunger again. Plant yourself next to the river and drink, drink, drink in the everlasting love, joy, peace, patience, kindness, goodness, gentleness, and self-control of the Lord.
>
> Prior to Courtside Ministries I was diseased with the American version of what I call C&E: Comfort and Entertainment for myself and family. I am thankful that enough of that finan-

cial and physical comfort was taken away so I could wake up. Several years later, the fervency for the Lord's work and eternal treasure has returned with greater power than ever before.

The majority of the reason I am back on fire for the Lord is because of Courtside Ministries.

No matter how the Lord has created you, the opportunities in the fields are truly abundant at the county courthouse. The only qualification to serve the Lord at Courtside is that you are a Jesus follower and have a willing heart. Whether you are outgoing or reserved, you can be used mightily by the Lord at your county courthouse by praying for those who are hurting.

Now that I volunteer at Courtside Ministries once a week, I am able to share about my faith in Christ more frequently. This has led to sharing my faith just about anywhere because my faith muscles are growing. My faith has increased so much because we have seen healings—physical and spiritual. Countless people have returned to the church, and many others have given their lives to Jesus. In addition, parents with children in prison weep with us as we weep with them about their children going to prison. We have prayed with countless couples who are walking into the court to get a divorce or are going through divorce proceedings with children. We have prayed with them to reconsider and we have seen fruit.

It does not matter what your gift is. The Lord will use you mightily at Courtside Ministries, whether you are a quiet prayer warrior, an outspoken evangelist, or an encourager. My spiritual gifts are firing on all cylinders like never before!

Come join us!

Enjoy more testimonies at courtsideministries.org.

What is so wonderful about Courtside Ministries is that it is not run by pastors. Sure, they may attend once in a while when the movement first comes to a nearby courthouse so they can check out the work and discern which members of their congregation would bless and be blessed most by bringing sympathy, forgiveness, healing, or salvation to four or five people a week. But doesn't Ephesians 4:11–12 tell us that "God gave tithers, members, and elders to pay for God's pastors to do works of service such as Courtside Ministries"? Of course not! In many ways, our conduct inverts the actual order of those verses. Paul actually writes,

> So Christ himself gave the apostles, the prophets, the evangelists, the pastors and teachers, to equip his people for works of service, so that the body of Christ may be built up. (Eph. 4:11–12)

Do you see the irony? Of course, we want our pastors to present the gospel at those crucial life-changing, life-reevaluating moments such as weddings or funerals, when our nonbelieving family members and friends may open their hearts to Christ. Yet Ephesians tells us the primary role of the pastor-teacher is to prepare God's people for works of service. Courtside Ministries aligns beautifully with Ephesians because it provides opportunities for non-ministers to do works of service.

Think of plaintiffs, defendants, judges, and lawyers—those struggling in the legal system—as a vast field ripe for harvest. God's workers are harvesting in the fields of Yeshua, laboring until His return. Then they look up and see a wonderful sight, like the people of Beth Shemesh:

> Now the people of Beth Shemesh were harvesting their wheat in the valley, and when they looked up and saw the ark, they rejoiced at the sight. The cart came to the field of Joshua of Beth Shemesh, and there it stopped beside a large rock. The people chopped up the wood of the cart and sacrificed the cows as a burnt offering to the LORD. (1 Sam. 6:13–14)

Notice that most of the workers are not priests, Levites, or royalty. Of course, the priests did their part in offering sacrifices, but the work was done primarily by people who were not ministers by profession.

Whether fishing or harvesting wheat, the biblical metaphor is consistent: God wants His fishermen and harvest workers where they can fish and reap bountifully. Often, that is outside the four walls of the church.

Could the Courtside move of God be one of the ways He is bringing into being another fulfillment of 2 Chronicles 7:14—"If my people, who are called by my name, will humble themselves and pray and seek my face and turn from their wicked ways, then I will hear from heaven, and I will forgive their sin and will heal their land"? Jesus sought to impact the legal system to reach Israel for the kingdom of God. In following the example He lived out for us, Courtside Ministries is impacting litigants, lawyers, and the legal system to reach the world for God's kingdom. And God is using non-lawyers to do so, to bring justice and mercy where it is needed!

THE WEAPONS OF OUR WARFARE

As we have seen from the victories in RLUIPA and Courtside Ministries, prayer is our ever crucial weapon in our legal-spiritual battles, but it is far from the only one. Paul calls the resources and gifts of the Wonderful Counselor "the weapons of our warfare" (2 Cor. 10:4 NKJV).

TOOLS AND RESOURCES USED BY GODLY LAWYERS INCLUDE:

1. Truth
2. Contracts/agreements
3. Paper trails
4. Witnesses
5. Research
6. Reason/persuasion
7. Warning letters
8. Arbitration/mediation
9. Lawsuits
10. Depositions
11. Motions
12. Briefs
13. Publicity
14. Financial support from believers
15. New legislation
16. Spiritual warfare weapons

Jesus equips us in spiritual warfare "against the rulers, against the authorities, against the powers of this dark world and against the spiritual forces of evil in the heavenly realms" (Eph. 6:12). In a lawsuit, we are not battling the other side or the judge. As Paul writes, "Our struggle is not against flesh and blood" (Eph. 6:12). Consequently, when confronted with a legal dispute, we must first discern what God's battle is, understand which legal tools apply (see above), and then focus on applying spiritual resources while using legal tools to assist us to win that battle. In other words, when you have a legal battle, first figure out God's objective, then review the resource list throughout this book and especially in Appendix C to see which apply to your battle or circumstance—and how your legal tools and spiritual resources combine to accomplish God's purposes. Whether you are a client, lawyer, a judge, or an advocate in any sense, I firmly believe you will be more victorious—as God considers victory—when you combine your spiritual resources with your legal weapons to fight legal battles God's way.

CHAPTER 4

GOD'S SPECIAL PEOPLE

Now we begin transitioning from teaching, preparing, and encouraging to outlining more direct ways all citizen-disciples can move forward to engage in battle, to carry on the work of our Wonderful Counselor in seeking justice and mercy. Although almost all human endeavors are impacted by law somehow, in order to take things from theory to practice, to show the nuances and interconnectivity of the law, we'll take a deep dive into one particular area. The same sort of in-depth exploration could be done for immigration, education, religious liberty, freedom of speech, or any number of areas. But this chapter will focus on one that the Bible and human law (frequently) call us as citizen-disciples to be responsible for: children.

Our Wonderful Counselor told us in strong terms not to put barriers between Him and children: "But Jesus said, 'Let the little children come to me and do not hinder them, for to such belongs the kingdom of heaven'" (Matt. 19:14 ESV). And, "But whoever causes one of these little ones who believe in me to sin, it would be better for him to have a great millstone fastened around his neck and to be drowned in the depth of the sea" (Matt. 18:6 ESV). Obviously children are of great worth to our Savior, and it goes without saying they should be for each of us.

Citizen-disciple, have you heard the legal standard to put "the best interest of the child first"? We should affirm that declaration; we should indeed hold our nations to that high and proper standard. But let us consider whether our laws actually put the child first. If they don't, what can we do to ensure they do? Even as we ask that question, let us pray: "Lord, is my heart soft, is it broken, concerning the burdens and dangers we have put on our little ones and the disregard we are showing to their needs? Help me, Lord, to have Your loving-kindness for Your children."

If any of the following occupations or categories apply to you, you have a special opportunity, a God-given responsibility, to influence, apply, or restore the "best interest of the child" standard in one or more areas of the law:

- media
- teachers
- pastors
- medical professionals (doctors and nurses)
- social workers
- union leaders
- counselors
- social media users
- lawyers
- judges
- legislators
- law students
- voters
- employers
- pro-choicers
- pro-lifers
- principals
- coaches
- parents or grandparents
- law enforcement
- donors

We will now consider how God wants you to use the law, truth, and your spiritual arsenal to help children in the following five areas:

1. abortion
2. adoption, foster care, and custody
3. school choice
4. higher education
5. sexual identity

ABORTION

Followers of Jesus who love the littlest of children have poured out their lives to save and protect them—and they will continue to do so. We honor and encourage pro-lifers throughout the world. God has given believers numerous ways to protect unborn children and influence their mothers to carry them to term. The importance of pregnancy centers, prayer, and electing pro-life legislators is already well known, so we will focus on three particular legal aspects of the struggle and one new idea:

- legal protection for pro-life ministries
- the importance of ultrasound
- how parental notification law is saving children

Then we will consider Qi Yuan, a game changer if God's people support it.

The Legal Battle to Protect Pro-Life Ministries

In the 1990s, American pro-choice activists almost succeeded in silencing Joe Scheidler, his Pro-Life Action League, and other defenders of unborn babies in the United States through legal action. A minuscule percentage of pro-lifers had engaged in violence against abortion clinics or abortionists. Under a relatively new federal law, the Racketeering and Corrupt Practices Act (RICO), the National Organization of Women (NOW) filed a federal lawsuit contending that nonviolent pro-lifers tacitly "conspired" with violent pro-life advocates for the same fully acknowledged objective—to close abortion facilities.

As conspirators, the suit alleged, all defendants shared liability for the damage inflicted by the violent few. NOW argued RICO did not require explicit agreement to use violence, but only implicit consent by nonviolent pro-lifers to the violence of others because they were all pursuing a common objective. NOW sued all the leading pro-life advocates in America in the Northern District Federal Court of Illinois located in Chicago. As the brutal and costly litigation proceeded, all the defendants—except Scheidler and his attorney, Tom Brejcha—surrendered to certain demands of NOW rather than bear the uncertainty and cost of continued litigation.

Brejcha was a successful partner in a large Chicago law firm when the litigation began. The partners kicked him out—some because they did not want to be associated with protecting the unborn, and others because they did not want to carry the IOUs for legal fees from Scheidler. So Brejcha founded the Thomas More Society to carry on the fight. He was battered and defeated on numerous occasions in the trial court and in the Seventh Circuit Court of Appeals. The first time the case went to the US Supreme Court, he lost again. But through grit and, no doubt, tears, Tom and Joe went to the Supreme Court twice more and prevailed. The litigation lasted over a decade, but God was faithful.

Those men—who are in my book of heroes of the law—

kept the door open for sidewalk counselors at abortion facilities throughout America, saving countless lives and touching multiplied thousands of consciences. They also protected civil rights in many other areas by obtaining a Supreme Court ruling that RICO did not apply to political social activism. They are heroes not because they won, but because they fought with all their strength and resources to defend the little ones. Dear reader, consider how many unborn lives would have been taken had it not been for these courageous souls and the citizen-disciples who backed them in prayer, finances, and encouragement. There are battles like this going on today, many more than we currently have resources to engage. If we read correctly the signs of the times, surely even a higher volume of important cases will come in the future. Our engagement as the Messiah's ambassadors in these battles between light and darkness is critical to the advancement of God's kingdom. Through us, our Wonderful Counselor desires to protect life, promote human flourishing, and seek the common good of all. It is up to us to understand and then to courageously engage.

Now the light is dawning: "The path of the righteous is like the morning sun, shining ever brighter till the full light of day" (Prov. 4:18). Abortions in the United States are in decline! American women are having significantly fewer abortions than in the past. Since 2010, the number of abortions nationwide has decreased by about 12 percent. This decline has been happening, slowly and steadily, for a quarter of a century: since 1990, the rate of abortions has fallen by more than a third, and the raw number of abortions has fallen by more than half.[1]

Most recently, the Thomas More Society has defended David Daleiden, the pro-life activist whose hidden camera interviews with Planned Parenthood executives have exposed their harvesting and selling of baby parts. Because of these revelations, some will rethink their plans and babies will be saved. Others will harden their hearts and continue to deceive themselves in believing that no innocent lives are being taken.

We must pray and stand in firm opposition to the killing of the children while loving and caring for the mothers. Of course, we as advocates of life must confront the truth that some mothers will choose to abort their unborn, that the availability of the "Morning After Pill" will continue even if certain laws prohibit it, and that *Roe v. Wade*, even if overruled by a new Supreme Court, will only send abortion law back to the states where many have legalized or will legalize it. Remember, the goal of the pro-life movement is not ultimately about law in the abstract, or even about reversing *Roe v. Wade*, but rather about saving lives by using law to educate and warn people that abortion takes innocent lives, to encourage adoption, and to impact our children to reject abortion and to embrace those who are distressed by an unwanted pregnancy.

Fighting for Ultrasound

Meet Vivian Maly, director of TLC Pregnancy Services in Elgin, Illinois. In 2013, that municipality moved to shut down a key service of her pro-woman, pro-life ministry. A certain Elgin alderwoman was offended by the presence of the TLC Pregnancy Center's mobile ultrasound unit, which was giving ultrasounds and other pregnancy information and support to women who responded to their offer of free services. Every Thursday from one to four o'clock in the afternoon while Elgin Larkin High School was in session, the Evangelical Free Church would welcome the TLC Mobile Unit to park in its lot immediately adjacent to the school. Over time, many young women got to see their unborn infants. Vivian told us that about 80 percent of abortion-minded women who view their child through ultrasound decide not to abort.

Numerous lives, not just in Elgin but throughout the world, were being saved by helping mothers see that their wombs were nurturing little people, not just "blobs," as some had been told. However, the alderwoman slipped through a zoning ordinance limiting "temporary land uses" (whatever that meant) to four times per year. Elgin then used that ordinance to shut down the TLC mobile ultrasound ministry at that crucial location. Vivian Maly decided to fight.

After failing to convince the Elgin legal department to relent, Mauck & Baker agreed to represent TLC in a federal lawsuit because of the evil consequences of the ordinance. As we prepared to litigate, we deployed one of our spiritual weapons. About twenty-six active or senior status judges preside in Illinois Northern District federal courts. New cases are randomly assigned to one of them. However, God is God over the courts just as much as He is over Congress. We instructed Vivian, and she enlisted ministry supporters to join us in praying that the case would be assigned to one specific judge. We knew this man to be a follower of Jesus fully committed to the Constitution, and thus protected from the pro-abortion politics and bias that typifies or intimidates some of the judiciary. (There are other God-honoring judges in the Northern District, but this is the one of which we were most sure and the only one we asked our Wonderful Counselor to select.) God provided "random" computerized assignment to that judge and the ordinance was ruled unconstitutional in a most encouraging way.

Parental Notification

The next series of cases is about how a unanimous Illinois Supreme Court (three Republicans and four Democrats) finally, after fifteen years of litigation, came to uphold the Illinois Parental Notification Act, *Hope Clinic v. Flores.* That Act requires, with some exceptions, notification of a parent or guardian prior to performance of an abortion on a woman under eighteen.

These victories for children came back to back—the ultrasound decision on July 11, 2013, and the parental notification decision on August 8, 2013, and both in Illinois. Were they random "coincidences" with no implications reaching beyond those directly affected? Or, when considered together, were they "God incidences," telling us something from God? Christian lawyers involved in both cases think God was sending a message through those cases. The reasoning of Judge Samuel Der Yeghiayan and the unanimous Illinois Supreme Court, and the resulting lives saved are lighting a path to saving even more lives!

In 2016, we got the results for abortions by adult women and minors for the year 2014, the first full year that parental notification was in force in Illinois. Although abortions in both groups declined from 2013, the decline in abortions by minors was remarkable. Three hundred to four hundred fewer babies were aborted by minors than if the decline in minor abortions had held to the same trend line as adult abortions. The only apparent reason for the encouraging decline in abortions by minors is that in 2013, parental notification was not law (was not enforced), but in 2014 it was enforced for half of the year. We thank God for the lives saved.

Similar parental notification laws are already in force in many states and could and should be adopted in every state and nation. What was powerful, and I believe prophetic, in both opinions was the rationale. In Vivian's TLC Pregnancy case, we had included the free speech and free exercise of religion constitutional rights of the pro-life counselors as legal bases for the court to rule in their favor. However, instead of following those legal pathways, the judge adopted what I now consider

our best argument. In the Parental Notification litigation, the proponents of the law argued—as had certainly been argued concerning similar laws everywhere—the rights of parents to protect their children. The courts had not found that rationale to be the most persuasive.

However, both the federal District Court and the Illinois Supreme Court focused on the rights of young women.

Judge Der Yeghiayan

Judge Samuel Der Yeghiayan wrote, "The Elgin ordinance infringes on the right of a woman to choose life." Likewise, the Illinois Supreme Court reasoned that young women, often immature, possibly confused, and certainly short on life experience, had a lawful right to wise counsel from someone who cared. What, through these and other legal decisions, is God showing us, His body, on our collective path to saving the lives of the littlest children? Certainly, education on what abortion constitutes for young women and their male partners is crucial. Pro-life activists through their use of ultrasound images of the child in the womb have been leading the way. How? By dispelling darkness with light, by combating ignorance with truth. These two court decisions have told us, in effect, "If you want to save babies, reach their mothers."

Qi Yuan Day

Many Christians realize abortion is murder, but many sixteen-year-old girls and their boyfriends mistakenly believe that life begins at birth. Our culture reinforces that misconception by birthday celebrations—a good event in most aspects—and our ubiquitous practices of connecting events, responsibilities, and privileges to our birthdates such as voting, bar mitzvah, and the drinking age, which are also good in most respects. One aspect of advancing God's kingdom through law is to think preventatively. If we can keep a case out of court or somehow influence public opinion in ways that will help prevent unrighteousness from occurring, then we should do our best to make that happen. Even so, as informed and concerned Christians, we should still seek to influence human laws to align as closely as possible to the heart of God through legal engagement. There is one practice that I will commend to you that will help correct misconceptions around when life starts: Qi Yuan Day.

Qi Yuan means "origin" or "beginning." The Chinese symbol simply means "day." However, the Chinese have for millennia dated a person's age from approximately the time of conception—adjusted for the vagaries of the Chinese calendar. Qi Yuan Day simplifies that by ascribing a Qi Yuan date to each person. So we have decided to adapt the Qi Yuan Day concept to an audience broader than China with our prayer to impact our cultures and thus save millions of lives.

How does Qi Yuan work?

Simply figure out the Qi Yuan Day—approximately 280 days prior to the birthdate or due date—and celebrate this day as when the life of the child actually began, or visit qiyuanday.com for an easy calculation. Put on your calendar the dates for those you would encourage, and as their Qi Yuan

PHOTO COURTESY OF QI YUAN COMPANY

YOU AT SIX WEEKS

Qi Yuan Greeting Card

Day approaches, send them a note (find samples at qiyuanday.com) reminding them of or celebrating the day their life began. The Qi Yuan Day website will show you many ways to be further involved or to involve others in encouraging our children, society, and nations to choose life. The goal is to reduce abortions by helping people acquire a clearer and more certain understanding that human life does not begin on the day of birth but on the day of conception. Observance of Qi Yuan Day will educate girls and boys who will become moms and dads that the mothers are nurturing a separate life. And this will help turn the hearts of the mothers to their children.

Consider the final verse of the Hebrew Scriptures prophesying the work of the coming Messiah, Wonderful Counselor: "He will turn the hearts of the fathers [and mothers] to the children, and the hearts of the children to their fathers [and mothers], lest I will come and strike the earth with a curse" (Mal. 4:6 NKJV). Malachi reminds us that fathers particularly, not just mothers, have a duty to the child they have procreated. And their duty is ultimately to God. Young men surprised by fatherhood have been known to panic and to pressure the woman to abort their child. For a man, who does not carry the child, the decision to abort may be easier. Many abortions could be avoided if the father agrees to support the pregnancy. Qi Yuan Day will help men, even from boyhood, realize their children are living persons at conception. These fathers, as taught by Qi Yuan Day and the Holy Spirit of Jesus, will be more likely to become men—supporting their co-procreator of life in protecting and nourishing the life of their child by avoiding abortion and encouraging other options such as adoption, as God "turn[s] the hearts of the fathers to the children."

Of course, God may impress you, dear reader, to do more than simply acknowledge Qi Yuan Day. Consider sending a Qi Yuan Day card to your pastor. Pastors, send them to the children in your congregation, those who attend your church camp or vacation Bible school. Parents and principals, this can be a good and godly component of sex education for your children and students in public and private schools, as well as a yearly reminder to them that you care about them especially.

We know our Wonderful Counselor loves us throughout our whole lives, and even before our conception: "Before I formed you in the womb I knew you, before you were born I set you apart" (Jer. 1:5).

A SPECIAL WORD TO PRO-CHOICE CHRISTIANS

You are a minority, and I know you feel it. Yet there are millions of you who are trying to follow Jesus. The large majority of people who call themselves Christians, particularly among evangelicals and Catholics, believe you are wrong—and some consider that you are ignorant or deceived.

Along with other pro-choicers, you care about the emotions and circumstances of the mother who has an unplanned pregnancy: sometimes fear, confusion, economic insecurity, and how it will impact her relationships. You also realize that many women, deprived of the legal option to abort, will pursue dangerous illegal alternatives. You are not "pro-abortion," in the sense that you think abortion is good. Rather, you are "pro-choice," because you believe legalized abortion affords better pathways for pregnant women. You agree with many pro-choice politicians who want abortion to be, as Hillary Clinton has said, "safe, legal, and rare."[2] Yet among pro-choicers, you are, I believe, also a minority. Those who lack belief in God, sin, judgment, or immortality have a less anguished path to a pro-choice position. To a significant degree, you are unwelcome or marginalized in both camps. However, God has you in a position like the Democrats on the Illinois Supreme Court, who in the same case where they voted to uphold Parental Notification also voted to recognize that the Illinois Constitution guaranteed freedom of abortion.

Your vigorous support of and implementation of Qi Yuan Day will likely be much more effective with pro-choicers than will the advocacy of pro-life Christians because you are more likely to be heard due to your shared values—though I ultimately urge you to become pro-life. Not only that, your advocacy of Qi Yuan Day will carry more influence with other pro-choice advocates and politicians who want to make abortion "legal, safe, and rare." You will help save lives.

Pastors and church leaders, you can appoint a congregational member or staff person to be your Qi Yuan Day Coordinator. Hopefully hesitancy of some pro-choicers to support Qi Yuan observers will help show pro-choicers that they fall short of their own standards of wanting abortion to be "rare." If they sincerely hope to make abortion rare, why oppose Qi Yuan Day? Some, we pray, will through truthful encounters realize they oppose their own standard and understand their need for the Savior. As with our attitude toward children, let us ask for softened hearts and loving-kindness toward those who disagree with us concerning abortion law, even toward abortionists.

ADOPTION, FOSTER CARE, AND CUSTODY

A child's biological parents are, generally speaking, best qualified and most motivated to raise their child well. Sadly, fallen humanity—whether through divorce, abandonment, abuse, illness, or death—often puts children in the hands of the government. Even though the world of child social care and placement abounds with dedicated and godly workers, the "best interest of the child" standard in foster care, adoption, and custodial cases has been weakened and is under assault.

Consider Erin, age one month, given up at birth by her single mother to Child Services for adoption. Two childless couples want to give Erin a loving home. Ben and Karen, both age thirty-one and married for nine years, are under final consideration, along with Mindy and Bill, age fifty-three and fifty-four, married for twenty years. Both wives have committed to be stay-at-home mothers, while both husbands have stable employment and, in the opinion of investigating social workers, would be great fathers. Other parental qualifications being equal, which couple will Child Services or the appropriate adoption agency choose? The answer is obvious to anyone who has experience in the field. (For nine years I was on the board of directors of a large child and family services organization.)

Erin deserves young parents who are more likely to have the energy to interact with her, to be in good health, and to still be alive and active during her childhood, adolescence, and early adulthood. In the best interest of Erin, Ben and Karen will be selected.

"Discrimination!" some cry. "Is not the only substantive difference between the couples age? And is not age discrimination illegal?" Well, yes. Placement with Ben and Karen is "discrimination," but the best interest of little Erin is the higher legal priority over the right of Mindy and Bill to "equal treatment," nondiscrimination under the law.

Now consider Kathy, age thirty days and also given up for adoption. Sara and Jill, both age twenty-eight, are in a stable same-sex relationship. They married soon after the Supreme Court in *Obergefell v. Hodges* required the state to sanction such unions. Mindy and Bill are back, still hoping to adopt.

Is it in Kathy's best interest to be adopted by two lesbians? Certainly, the age factor weighs in favor of Sara and Jill. However, a census-based study of 20 percent of the entire Canadian population concluded:

> Children living with gay and lesbian families in 2006 were about 65 percent as likely to graduate compared to children living in opposite sex marriage families. . . . A breakdown of performance by the sex of the child shows a more dramatic result. Daughters of gay parents are only 15 percent as likely to graduate high school while daughters of lesbian parents are 45 percent as likely to graduate.[3]

Another major study shows that adults who were raised by a lesbian mother had, as they were growing up, greater instances of sexual abuse. As adults, they also were more prone to suicidal thoughts, drug use, unemployment, and other key measures of a dysfunctional life.[4] (I commend to you the interactive graphics at familystructurestudies.com.)

So should the child placement officials be able to weigh risks of the age of Mindy and Bill against the risks of the sexuality of

Sara and Jill to determine the best interest for Kathy's life? If the child's best interest is our goal, then certainly! Citizen-disciples should acknowledge that in our fallen world, factors such as age, income, health, or addictions will sometimes point away from heterosexual adopters and in favor of same-sex couples. Gay and lesbian activists should acknowledge that gay parenting poses many special risks to children, and that those risks should be carefully weighed in any adoption, custody, or foster care determination.

IN MANY STATES, THE BEST INTEREST OF THE CHILD HAS BEEN OVERRIDDEN BY POLITICAL CORRECTNESS.

However, in Illinois, and probably in other "progressive" states and nations, the best interest of the child has been overridden by political correctness. When Illinois legalized civil unions in 2011, Attorney General Lisa Madigan, the state's highest elected law enforcement official, sent an edict to child placement agencies throughout Illinois, informing them that they were places of public accommodation and that they violated the law if they discriminated based on the marital status of a foster, adoptive, or custodial parent. Violators would face legal penalties. A warning like that forced immediate compliance because a charge of "unlawful discrimination" from the State could put an agency out of business.

For these and similar reasons, Catholic Charities exited all child social care throughout Illinois. All the other secular and purportedly faith-based agencies refused to challenge what I consider legalized and officially sanctioned child endangerment. No one went to court to assert that Kathy and other children should be placed according to their best interest and not to fall victim to the "political correctness" *du jour*. Thousands of Illinois children—and only God knows how many across the world—are exposed to greater and unnecessary risks throughout childhood because some laws mandate subordination of their best interests by ignorance, even willful ignorance, of the risks that gay parenting or single parenting instead of traditional parenting poses.

Why is the best interest standard weakening? At least four reasons explain why:

1. Satan hates children. I believe he was behind the murder by Pharaoh of the Hebrew boys (see Ex. 1:15–16, 22) and Herod's slaughter of the innocents when the Messiah was born (see Matt. 2:16–18).

2. Children have no money, no vote, and insufficient advocacy. Teachers' union officials and deficit-spending politicians have more to fear from their special-interest constituencies than they do from five-year-olds.

3. God's people perish for lack of knowledge. Either we don't know what to do or we do but fail to do it. We have not allowed the Lord to shape us as the citizen-disciples He would have us be. He is warning us: "My people are destroyed from lack of knowledge. 'Because you have rejected knowledge, I also reject you as my priests; because you have ignored the law of your God, I also will ignore your children'" (Hos. 4:6).

4. When a nation fails to protect unborn children, it is easier to dismiss thinking that children already born merit special concern.

This book was written, in part, to help us as citizen-disciples understand and use the law to address the prior four reasons.

Here's what we all can do:

Campaign and vote for the best interests of children. Sadly, I've heard many reports that followers of Jesus register to vote and cast ballots at about the same percentage as non-Christians. Why would we fail to exercise our God-given privilege to bring justice and mercy to our legal and political systems? Certainly, sin is one answer. I have heard Christians proclaim, "I won't vote for ____ because he's a liar and I won't vote for ____ because she's a liar." By not voting, we are shirking our responsibilities to our children. Liar or not, candidates differ. Jesus is not running for office, and when He returns, His return will not be a response to a plebiscite. Meanwhile, voting is not about you "polluting yourself" by supporting impure candidates. While keeping a clear conscience before God must be worked out by each individual Christian as they vote, it's about deciding who will be best for children and others.

Support broad-based "best interest of the child" legislations. Discern which legislations seek the interests of children over the rights of adoptive, custodial, or foster parents and support them as best as you can.

Get informed about the legal battles in your state and pray that the courts and attorneys will fight for children's best interests. Of course, as parents, grandparents, pastors, lawyers, social workers, teachers, and others involved with children, you can have more direct involvement in seeking what is best for the children in your life. You may be thinking, *But, Attorney Mauck, I don't think you understand. If I stand up for children against abortion, adoption by homosexuals, and so forth, I could lose my job, my friends, my congregation, or my family.* Well, yes. You could. Let us remember what Revelation 12:11 says about the faithful: "They triumphed over him by the blood of the Lamb and by the word of their testimony; *they did not love their lives so much as to shrink from death*" (emphasis added). And what Jesus said while teaching about the cost of being His disciple: "Anyone who loves their father or mother more than me is not worthy of me; anyone who loves their son or daughter more than me is not worthy of me. Whoever does not take up their cross and follow me is not worthy of me. Whoever finds their life will lose it, and whoever loses their life for my sake will find it" (Matt. 10:37–39). As long as fear of loss of any kind keeps us from obeying God's Word, we are ineffective—and ultimately unfulfilled.

In his book, *Is Justice Possible?* Moody Bible Institute president Dr. Paul Nyquist reflects:

[The role of government in creating and maintaining an adequate safety net] is a justice issue to God. Rulers, leaders, and judges have a responsibility before God to take up the cause of the poor, for usually those on the bottom shelves of our society suffer the most. In our country, the fastest growing segment of the poor are children. Across our land, despite our wealth, 20 percent of our children live below the poverty line—struggling to gain adequate nutrition, health care, housing, and schooling. We tend to blame the poor for their poverty. Children cannot be blamed for their poverty. They just need help.[5]

SCHOOL CHOICE

The people who love children most, who will work and sacrifice for their well-being including receiving proper education, are Mom and Dad. We are not saying many principals, teachers, and politicians do not care deeply. They do. However, in most cases, the parents care more because:

- their child is their own;
- they've known and nurtured the child since birth (or rather, since Qi Yuan Day);
- their concern is focused on a particular child, and not a classroom of fifteen or twenty-five;
- their relationship with the child extends, hopefully, for a lifetime, not for only a year or two;
- their relationship and bonding is based on the natural love God has given parents for their children; and
- to a significant degree, the future well-being of parents is still connected to the child's success.

Nevertheless, many politicians have largely resisted and restricted voucher and charter school programs that would empower parents of public school students with the school choices that, with remarkable consistency, deliver better education.

Many teachers' unions predictably press for more money "in the best interest of the children," but somehow the extra funding seems to go to the teachers while student test scores stagnate or decline. Meanwhile, the pension plans with promises of public funding loom like ravenous beasts waiting to devour the earnings of those very children when they get old enough to be fitted with the shackles that irresponsible lawmakers have forged for their future bondage. Cami Anderson, a former superintendent of Newark Public Schools, in a March 21, 2016, *Wall Street Journal* op-ed, decried union staffers who zealously defended a "quality blind" teacher tenure system that traded teacher job security over the future of children. My opinion and the essence of hers is that "the best interest of the child" has been subordinated to "the best interest of the teachers' union."

In 2002, the Supreme Court by a five-to-four vote upheld

the legality of Ohio's voucher plan to promote school choice.[6] While this decision allowed school choice to go forward, it left many questions open, and the battle still rages. The website for National School Choice Week (see schoolchoiceweek.com) lists over a dozen resources to help believers engage in the legal struggle to allow school choice by parents for their children.

Are you or do you know folks in the public education system? Frankly, privatization through school choice may require some teachers and administrators to find new jobs— particularly if they are mediocre, inefficient, or lazy. However, the diligent and talented teacher or administrator may well receive a dual blessing from an increase in school choice:

1. satisfaction in seeing more children and young people better educated; and
2. greater compensation and recognition as increased competition rewards those who teach best.

Nevertheless, some diligent and talented public school teachers may face unemployment or decreased income. Let us recall that the call to discipleship is indeed costly, and that some followers of Jesus will endure great loss as a result of remaining faithful to Him (see Luke 14:26–27). And to them may our Wonderful Counselor bring to mind Matthew 6:25, "Therefore I tell you, do not worry about your life, what you will eat or drink; or about your body, what you will wear. Is not life more than food, and the body more than clothes?" and 6:33, "But seek first his kingdom and his righteousness, and all these things will be given to you as well."

HIGHER EDUCATION

Many people in our society recognize the advantages of receiving higher education. Unfortunately, three big sins abound in this area, which either limit the opportunities young people have in pursuing further education, or place them at a disadvantage in life after completing a higher education degree.

First, public subsidies for this sector via our income tax laws have contributed to massive increases in what colleges charge to educate. Thus, they have saddled graduates—and those unable to complete college—with a huge amount of debt, causing many to postpone marriage and having children.

Second, restriction of Bible schools through accreditation laws by about half of the states has hurt many students, depriving them of a far less expensive option and keeping them from learning more about God and achieving spiritual growth.

Bible colleges offer an affordable education, but many are prevented by state education boards from award degrees. This is odd, considering that Bible colleges have an illustrious history in the United States. For instance, Congregationalist ministers founded Yale to equip young men for pastoral ministry. But many Bible colleges today are being relegated to second-class status. States should not impose accreditation requirements onto Bible schools for at least two reasons: First, the government is not competent to evaluate the quality of a bachelor's degree in evangelism or a master's in theology. Second, politicians often succumb to the temptation to insert conditions for accreditation designed to benefit the politician and his or her constituency rather than the students or the school.[7]

Third, our higher educational system is abusing our young people by keeping them from wrestling with controversial issues. As Michael Bloomberg, former mayor of New York, and

Charles Koch, conservative activist, wrote in a *Wall Street Journal* op-ed: "Colleges are increasingly shielding students from any idea that could cause discomfort or offense. Yet without the freedom to offend, freedom of expression, as author Salman Rushdie once observed, 'ceases to exist.'"[8]

We can put the best interest of students first by bringing costs down or limiting increases through increased competition from more schools, including Bible colleges. Ask.com indicates there are over 1,200 Bible schools and colleges in the United States. This would include both state-approved and non-approved institutions. Freeing these schools to compete more fully would impact education positively.

As parents, we should send our children to schools that foster broad diversity of opinions and healthy debate. As alumni, we should stop giving to our almae matres unless they champion freedom of expression on campus. Individual alumni can set up charitable educational trusts to foster academic freedom. These trusts can compete with the alma mater for donations and bequests accumulating funds to sponsor speakers expressing or courses containing ideas that will challenge closed-minded students and institutions. If a particular school won't protect the right of its students to consider unpopular viewpoints, then the trustees of alumni trusts should have guidelines to allow the funds to be spent at other schools or elsewhere for educational diversity. Why support schools that prevent students from considering the values we cherish?

An attorney knowledgeable in estates, trusts, and foundations can help you set up such trusts or other legal mechanisms to ensure the money and assets from your life's work for God are not used against God's kingdom. If several alumni can join you, you will probably be more effective. The Christian Legal Society can help you find such an attorney. If you have an attorney who tries to dissuade you from putting godly conditions on gifts—currently or posthumously—to colleges or universities or ministries, then get a new attorney. What is more important: "loyalty" for the sake of personal identity to a school that undermines godly principles, or support of edifying, kingdom-building education no matter where it occurs? While we are at it, here are two provisions from my will that every believer should prayerfully consider including in their own testamentary planning (including living trusts):

> I, JOHN W. MAUCK, of Evanston, Illinois, being of sound disposing mind and memory, and realizing the uncertainty of this life, and with full confidence and trust in my Lord and Savior, Jesus Christ, in His death on the cross and shed blood as an atonement for my sins, and knowing that by faith in His sacrifice on the cross for me I now have eternal life, do hereby make, publish and declare the following to be my Last Will & Testament, hereby revoking all former Wills and Codicils thereto, if any, by me made. My fondest hope and prayer and that of my wife, Rosemary, is that all of our descendants and their spouses will spend eternity with us accepting the life Jesus has made possible. . . .
>
> I believe same-sex marriages pose great risk to children, especially in the child custody dispute, adoption and foster care context. I also believe that homosexual conduct deeply harms those engaged in it and is thus sinful as set forth in Romans 1 and other scriptures. Therefore, if prior to the time of distribution of my estate _____Church has ever allowed same-sex couples to marry on its premises or under its auspices or if it has hired any Pastor, youth leader, or counselor who is in a same-sex marriage or civil union or is unrepentant in homosexual conduct, said bequest to _____Church shall be void and the six percent (6%) share intended for it shall be added pro rata to the share of the other Christian organizations named above.

While this shows what I have done in regard to my church, the same could be done for gifts intended for other faith-based educational institutions.

SEXUAL IDENTITY

How do we as followers of Jesus and believers in God's Word respond to unprecedented legal attacks against biblical sexual ethics? Those attacks have succeeded in court declarations that laws limiting marriage to a man and woman "discriminate," thus mandating social and legal approval of same-sex "marriage." More than just seeking freedom for gay/lesbian conduct and marriage, those attacks are morphing into demands that those who believe such conduct and marriage are sinful and harmful to others must change their opinions, shut their mouths, or even violate their consciences by facilitating actions that further that agenda. Well-known examples are the requiring of wedding photographers and wedding cake bakers to help celebrate those weddings despite moral opposition to same-sex unions or convictions that participation is an endorsement of a lifestyle that negatively impacts young people.

Importantly, numerous resources are being marshaled by Christian legal organizations and other Christian groups to inform the public and citizen-disciples of the danger to rights of conscience and free exercise of religion. However, remember that a team that plays only defense will usually lose and, at best, will end up with a nil-nil draw.

So let us ask a concomitant and arguably more important question: how can believers, godly lawyers and judges, truth seekers, and lovers of truth use these attacks to:

1. help confused youth;

2. proclaim God's love to gays, lesbians, and others of
varying sexual attractions or choices; and

3. build God's kingdom?

To answer that question partially, we will examine one particular target of the gay/lesbian agenda: reparative therapy for
those who have unwanted same-sex attractions.

"Reparative therapy" is counseling—clinical or pastoral—
that helps a person with those attractions understand themselves, overcome unwanted desires, reorient their desires,
or adjust to a healthy celibate life. God cares deeply about
those who are sexually wounded, dysfunctional, disoriented,
abused, and confused. Do we? Teenagers in particular need
loving guidance from parents, school counselors, pastors, and
psychologists because:

1. they are hit by raging hormones;
2. they are inexperienced and vulnerable; and
3. predators, pressure from peers, and the Internet instill
confusion and seek to seduce and exploit them.

Such counseling is sought primarily by people, both minors
and adults, who do not want or are ambivalent about their
same-sex attractions. Yet amid this great need of teenagers for
our help, the gay-lesbian agenda has targeted those involved in
reparative therapy to prohibit their work.

For example, in 2012 the American Psychological Association
(APA) produced a study asserting that "efforts to change sexual
orientation have not been shown to be effective or safe."[9] In other
words, the APA and studies that agreed with its conclusion are
claiming that they have "truth," which would require laws—in

the best interest of children and others—to prohibit reparative therapy. The study disregards the experiences of Christian psychologists specializing in reparative therapy, who report successes in helping those with unwanted same-sex attractions to reorient to heterosexuality or reduce unwanted same-sex attractions.[10] Stanton Jones, professor of psychology and core studies at Wheaton College, requested, along with other experienced Christian counselors, to be included on the committee that produced the report.[11] They were excluded. Thus, the study's objectivity and commitment to truth over political correctness is suspect. For those who care about truth regarding whether change in one's sexual orientation is possible, check out the documentary "Such Were Some of You" by David Foster.[12]

I find irony in those who urge "latent homosexuals" to "come out of the closet" while denying that those with unwanted gay urges can reorient their sexual attractions. Is it possible that perhaps hundreds of thousands of latent homosexuals abound, but that "latent heterosexuals" do not exist? Despite the dearth of evidence that homosexual orientation is inevitable and thus unalterable, and despite the many testimonies of lives changed out of the gay lifestyle through therapy or appeal to Jesus, the crusade to prohibit reparative therapy is well underway. I will describe the strategy of those seeking to prevent reparative therapy, and then we will consider how we can use our spiritual and legal weapons to accomplish God's purposes. The campaign to prohibit reparative therapy appears to be patterned on strategy to legalize homosexual marriage: use the states with heavy liberal legislative majorities to pass new laws. If the public should overrule the legislature by referendum, then use the courts to overrule the people.

In a fashion similar to the gay marriage campaign, reparative therapy bans have been enacted in Massachusetts, New Jersey, California, and Illinois as of 2017, with legislation pending in a number of states. The Illinois law is aggressive. Whereas all the laws provide penalties for licensed counselors—doctors, psychologists, school counselors, and others who offer reparative therapy—Illinois has put pastors at risk. It declares "consumer fraud" for any person "in commerce" who refers to homosexuality as a "disorder." The interpretation of "in commerce" has been broadened over time and now threatens to engulf anyone who is paid for counseling. Thus, a salaried pastor who is not licensed by Illinois but whose duties include counseling visitors or even members with unwanted same-sex attractions could be sued for consumer fraud were he or she to refer to homosexual conduct as sin and thus a "disorder." Of course, under the law the same pastors would be free to counsel or teach, "God approves of your homosexual conduct and does not want you to try to change your orientation." What a double standard.

We must again remember that our battle is not against gay or lesbian people but on behalf of all people. Paul taught, "For our struggle is not against flesh and blood, but against the rulers, against the authorities, against the powers of this dark world and against the spiritual forces of evil in the heavenly realms" (Eph. 6:12). If we hold an ungodly attitude toward those who engage in homosexual activities and promote that lifestyle, we will be ineffective.

Truth and love must be employed in and out of court—particularly toward young people who want help. The courts and pro-choicers—who prefer to be called "pro-choice" rather than "pro-abortion"—have always prioritized a "woman's right to choose." As I explained in the previous section about abortion that women have the right to information about their pregnancies, so I propose that each person has the right to be fully informed regarding the many aspects and consequences of sexual behavior—emotional, spiritual, social, medical—and about issues relating to identity, celibacy, and monogamy. If a sixteen-year-old young woman has started a sexual relationship with another young woman, why should the law take away her right to seek counsel from her pastor, doctor, mother, or high school adviser?

In ruling on whether abortionists could argue on behalf of and represent the rights of young women to choose abortion, the US Supreme Court ruled that "it generally is appropriate to allow a physician to assert the right of women patients as against governmental interference with the abortion decision."[13]

Following the principle established in the *Wulff* case, we felt that it was fully appropriate for pastors to argue for the rights of young people in their churches to choose to request pastoral counseling. That is the position we took in *Pastors Protecting Youth et al. v. Lisa Madigan, Illinois Attorney General, in her Official Capacity*, which we filed in August 2016. Of course, we also argued for the free speech and free exercise of religion rights of pastors and presented those legal theories. Our legal objective was to obtain a court order (a "Declarative Judgment") declaring that the law does not encompass pastors, or that the law does apply to pastors but is invalid as so applied because the constitutional rights of the counselees and the pastors outweigh the regulatory interests of the state.

We thank God that in February 2017 Federal District Court Judge Ronald Guzmán ruled that pastors who were salaried to counsel as part of the normal course of their pastoral duties were not "in commerce" and thus not subject to penalties under the law banning reparative therapy. Because the judge explained his reasoning for their exclusion from liabilities under the new law, we and our clients, an association of evangelical pastors, fully agreed with Judge Guzmán's dismissal of the suit "for lack of standing"—that is, he effectively ruled that there was no legal way the statute prohibited pastors from counseling that homosexual conduct was sinful and could be overcome with Jesus' help. We believe legal victories like this, multiplied across America and indeed across the world, will ultimately help struggling adolescents find God's path.

Thus, one of our constant and powerful spiritual weapons in the arena of sexual identity is truth. Recently, two leading scholars on mental health and sexuality, Dr. Lawrence Mayer and Dr. Paul McHugh at Johns Hopkins, released a 143-page report, "Sexuality and Gender," published in the fall 2016 edition of *The New Atlantis*, a widely respected "Journal of Technology and Society." In the preface, Dr. Mayer dedicated the report "first to the LGBT community, which bears a disproportionate rate of mental health problems compared to the population as a whole. We must find ways to relieve their suffering!" The report digests and discusses over 200 peer-reviewed studies, what such research concludes, and where some politically correct ideas on sexual identity lack scientific foundation. For example, the report refutes the currently popular understanding that "gay people are born that way," showing that the studies do not support that assertion and concludes that whether homosexual attraction as orientation develops or is caused is still unproven. And whether or not a "gay gene" is proven to exist does not mean people are not responsible for their sinful actions.

I believe that simple truth has dramatic implications:

- because homosexual behavior is not inevitable, it, and even same-sex attraction, can be overcome;

• efforts to help people with unwanted same-sex attraction should be allowed, not criminalized or penalized.

The LGBT Watershed Moment

With its legal victory in *Obergefell* requiring all states to sanction same-sex marriage, the LGBT movement has arrived at a watershed moment, a moment of truth. Such a moment occurs at the end of a battle or struggle and tests the character of the victor.

I recently had the privilege of giving interviews to two publications reaching largely gays, lesbians, and those supporting their agenda. As religious liberty litigators, we reach out to these media with the hope that our Jesus-centered message will impact some hearts. The interviews both concerned our Pastors Protecting Youth litigation to protect the freedom of pastors to speak truth without government interference to those struggling with same-sex attractions. This is a paraphrase of what I essentially said to both reporters:

> This is a watershed moment for gays and lesbians. Many have felt they have struggled for years, even centuries, against hatred, discrimination, and unjust laws. Although Jesus teaches His disciples to hate the sin but love the sinner, certainly many of His followers have hated those who engage in homosexual practice despite that teaching. However, the legal persecution gays and lesbians have experienced is effectively over. Homosexual conduct has been de facto legal for fifty years and legalized by the Supreme Court throughout the US for about fifteen years. Now with *Obergefell*, gay marriage is lawful throughout the US.
>
> Will the ascendant LGBT movement, formerly persecuted, now become the persecutors penalizing pastors who still teach that homosexual conduct is sin, removing "accreditation" from private schools that deny married student housing or health insurance to same-sex couples?

I received the same response from each reporter: a quivering voice and what seemed to be a holding back of tears. I assumed they both had invested years in the battle for gay equality and were experiencing an emotional moment where they could reexamine the character of the movement and their own character—triumphalism or humility.

I commend the challenge I presented those reporters to each reader who agrees that our battle is not against "flesh and blood, but against the rulers, against the authorities, against the powers of this dark world and against the spiritual forces of evil in the heavenly realms" (Eph. 6:12). No matter whether our values are accepted in society or not, let us be characterized by humility. Please refer to the lists of spiritual resources and weapons in Appendix C. Consider which of these you can employ to support our legal battle, to preserve the right of young people to get godly counsel, or to help a person struggling with sexual identity. Then use the resources God has given us!

Our journey has taken us through the laws affecting our children in the five areas of abortion, adoption and foster care, school choice, higher education, and sexual identity—and how we must engage. We could go on and discuss how minimum wage laws devastate youth—particularly inner-city young men—because increased minimum wages limit the number of entry-level workers that employers can hire. As a result, fewer inner-city youth are developing key life skills. Consequently, some are turning to gang violence and drug dealing. We could also discuss how our deficit spending continues to pile up debt on our own children, but I trust you get the point: we must litigate for rulings and fight for laws that help or protect our youth. Not everyone is equipped to fight for these issues within the legislative realm. But you, dear reader, can at least pray for God's will to be accomplished in these areas. Let us see clearly how children are affected in all these areas and fight for justice and mercy to the extent that we can.

CHAPTER 5

OUR FUTURE

Having come to understand God's work through the law and the urgent needs of the day, we are left with three choices: (1) ignore things; (2) lament, maybe complain, yet perhaps do nothing; or (3) prayerfully engage. Let's consider our response.

NOW WHAT?

Paul writes to the Romans, "Where sin increased, grace increased all the more" (5:20). As we watch events in these days of terror, anger, and "fake news," it is easy to see the sin. But our Wonderful Counselor wants us to be not only resisters of the evil that assails us, but also dispensers of the grace He is causing to increase abundantly.

There is a bigger story, and you are part of it. There is a bigger world, and laws and the legal system are but a component within God's metanarrative. Our Extraordinary Strategist has shown us on multiple levels how we are to love justice, dispense mercy, and walk humbly with Him through:

- our individual and collective identities
- our knowledge of His law
- our occupation or avocation
- our gifts and spiritual weaponry
- caring for children
- following directions from Him

He has shown us that, yes, each of us, living out our identity as His beloved sons and daughters, can serve Him through engaging the law and lawyers. And if you labor for God, you are never unemployed.

OUR WONDERFUL COUNSELOR WANTS US TO BE NOT ONLY RESISTERS OF EVIL THAT ASSAILS US, BUT ALSO DISPENSERS OF THE GRACE HE IS CAUSING TO INCREASE ABUNDANTLY.

Our children—do they direct our ministry? Most certainly! God is calling us to protect, teach, and spiritually equip our adopted and natural children and the children in our congregations, communities, and world. Through prayer we can discern a few, and sometimes many, ways that we can marshal what God has given us, not only to rescue our children, but also to help them become the vanguard of the Messiah's return.

Our Wonderful Counselor's special direction for each of us is well summarized by Paul in Ephesians 2:10: "For we are God's handiwork, created in Christ Jesus to do good works, which God prepared in advance for us to do."

YOUR PLACE IN HIS WORK

Hopefully by now you are convinced that lawyers are not the only ones who can engage and impact the legal system. If you still believe that only lawyers can do legal work, it is probably because you have succumbed to a more problematic fallacy: the false dichotomy of "clergy" and "laity," "ministers" and "non-ministers."

Let me explain Ephesians 2:10 and the common objection presented by addressing a vocabulary, paradigm, and way of thinking that still confuses God's people and inhibits us from embracing our roles as citizen-disciples—whether we are sanitation workers, lawyers, salespeople, graphic designers, or any other non-full-time ministry workers. I touched on the clergy-laity fallacy earlier when I commended the Courtside Ministries model in comparison to our pastors ministering at weddings and funerals. Now we will revisit that fallacy in detail from the viewpoint of you, the citizen-disciple who has a busy life. If you can understand how the clergy-laity fallacy has held us back in pursuing more ardently God's call on our lives, then I hope you will see that perceiving a division between lawyers and non-lawyers can beget an equally harmful fallacy.

From Catholic tradition and elements of the Reformation tradition that are with us today, we get the misconception that some are selected for God's work while others are not. Although many teachers in both traditions have sought to correct this misconception, confusion still abounds. Ephesians 4:11–13 teaches,

> So Christ himself gave the apostles, the prophets, the evangelists, the pastors and teachers, to equip his people for works of service, so that the body of Christ may be built up until we all reach unity in the faith and in the knowledge of the Son of God and become mature, attaining to the whole measure of the fullness of Christ.

Ephesians tells us we are either equippers or those being equipped—not "clergy" or "laity," not ministers or church members. The misconception that some are called to ministry while others are not can also lead believers to think that legal battles are strictly for lawyers, when in fact God wants us all to be engaged, to some extent, in the legal matters we have already considered such as abortion, protecting children and marriage, or prayer and financial support for civil liberty defenders. I will illustrate first with a real-life example and then with a parable that the confusion indeed persists and explain how we should rethink, repent of, and correct our faulty understanding.

Who Are the Ministers?

A church I know has been faithfully teaching God's Word for 150 years. For most of those years, I am told, it has designated 20 percent or more of its budget to support missions. Recently, leaders put together a 52-week prayer guide to educate their members on the ministries they support financially and so they could also support and advance spiritually the work of these ministries to build the kingdom. Their ministries included church planters risking their lives in Muslim countries, medical missionaries in developing nations, outreaches to male prostitutes in Chicago, and church-sponsored help to the poor such as the "deacons' clothes closet." Are prayer guides for such ministries good? Absolutely! But do they reflect a blind spot that many churches have? Yes.

This particular church and the large majority of churches I work with have the same blind spot: they pray and highlight the testimonials of missionaries and church-sponsored ministries far more than they do for the vast majority in the congregation who are artists, retired people, homemakers, bankers, and others. Is it any wonder that the implicit message "you are laity, not God's workers" persists so widely? Some "laypeople" do not do God's work in building the kingdom because they are confused, thinking kingdom work is only for the elders and other full-time ministry workers. Other "laypeople" use their status as an excuse not to do God's work or to do less than they are capable of. Yet others feel they lack the time to perform "ministry work." Perhaps they do not realize that the Father of eternity can create time when we put His kingdom first (Matt. 6:28–34).

Ellen and Her Sisters: A Parable

A Christian couple had four daughters. Each loved God, and they all loved each other. The eldest daughter had five children and was busy as a stay-at-home mom, raising them to love God. The second became a doctor working in geriatrics in an affluent suburban community. The third daughter taught in a public middle school in a blue-collar neighborhood of a large city. When Ellen, the youngest, and her husband became missionaries to indigenous people in Mexico, the entire family rejoiced, gladly supporting them financially as their work did not generate income. Every month, her parents sent an email to the other daughters, detailing Ellen's prayer needs: her health, her marriage, her conflict with missionary supervisors, her need to communicate better with uninterested tribal leaders or hostile governmental authorities, and so on. All the other daughters prayed for Ellen and her needs.

After several years, the three older daughters came to the parents with a question: "Mom and Dad, you raised us to believe we *all* were God's workers. We *all* have marriage issues, problems in our work, conflicts at church, and so many challenges in presenting the gospel to our children, our geriatric patients, and our students. One of us was threatened with dismissal just for saying 'Merry Christmas' to her students! At least Ellen can say 'Feliz Navidad' without fear. We all are trying to serve the Lord and build God's kingdom. Your prayer reminders for Ellen have begun to make us feel our work for God is less important than Ellen's. We are confused and grieved. Is she in ministry more than the rest of us? Should not we all have prayer bulletins sent to the whole family?"

Here is a prayer we can offer up as we wrestle with our place in serving the kingdom:

> Wonderful Counselor, forgive me for lack of faith or for allowing laziness or fear to keep me from living out my calling as Your ambassador. Help me overcome these barriers by the strength that comes from Your joy and the sure understanding that You have chosen me for special work in Your kingdom. I thank You that You delight to guide my steps on to the particular path You have ordained for me. I seek the path You want me to take. Let my heart, will, and mind be fully aligned with Your plan for me, my Counselor and Savior. Amen.

Hopefully this isn't the first discussion you've heard about the fallacy of the clergy-laity divide. However, this book might be the first time you've heard about the fallacy of the lawyer-non-lawyer divide when it comes to advancing God's kingdom through the law. As we have discussed throughout this book, lawyers certainly play a critical role in advancing God's kingdom to promote life, human flourishing, and the common good. Yet they cannot do it alone—nor should they! By now you understand your role as a citizen-disciple. Dear reader, please confirm to our Wonderful Counselor right now that your citizenship is an integral part of your discipleship, and that fighting legal battles is a part of your role as Christ's soldier.

WHAT DOES VICTORY LOOK LIKE?

To help us consider what our victory looks like, we should first note what it is *not*.

Back in the 1980s, I heard about a well-known rabbi who was teaching on Jewish-Christian relationships to a mixed audience of Christians and Jews. Having learned that the rabbi had New Testament scholarship credentials, I had lots of questions and was particularly curious about why he did not believe Jesus was the Messiah. So I invited him to meet with a small group of believers at my home. His presentation was completely respectful of Christianity.

Toward the end of that evening, I asked him directly, "Rabbi, why don't you believe in Jesus?" He dodged the question twice, but in the same tone of respect I persisted. Finally, he gave a direct, and I believe sincere, response: "I don't believe in Jesus because I see Christianity as a religion of triumphalism." Although he did not elaborate, I've given his answer much thought and want to explain what I think this particular objection to the gospel means and how we can learn from it and better define the victory of God.

First, the rabbi was making the common quasi-mistake of judging the Christian religion by the followers of Jesus, instead of dealing with who Jesus is, His teaching, and His resurrection. Certainly Christians fall short of Jesus' example all the time, in many ways. So if he wants to consider what it means to be a follower of Jesus, he should ultimately focus on Him. Second, I characterize his mistake not as total but as quasi because he was partly right. Jesus taught us, "No good tree bears bad fruit, nor does a bad tree bear good fruit. Each tree is recognized by its own fruit. People do not pick figs from thorn bushes, or grapes from briers" (Luke 6:43–44). Our rabbi acquaintance properly considered evidence of the truth of Christianity and all who profess to follow Yeshua by the results their lives produced.

So here are some aspects of triumphalism that some of us express with a prideful attitude. Please be sensitive to the reality that the sin of triumphalism is not simply directed toward the historic sibling rival of Christianity (that is, Judaism), but also to other groups such as Muslims or secularists who may feel that Christians, Christian America, or "Christendom" are trying to dominate them. These manifestations keep nonbelievers from seeing Jesus:

1. The belief that Christians are better than nonbelievers
2. Christianity has more adherents than other religions
3. Christians control American law, and many American presidents have been Christians
4. Our laws will control your moral conduct
5. The church has replaced Israel

I have not listed these examples of triumphalism to show how the perceptions of our critics may be mistaken, but rather to help us realize how Christians and Christianity are perceived by many and for us to think about which aspects of their perceptions are true so we can change our behaviors, laws, and legal agendas that lead to those perceptions. Should our public schools teach the superiority of Christianity? Absolutely not! Neither should they teach that Islam, Communism, or atheism are, either. Should they educate our children on what these and other groups believe? Certainly! For example, although the courts have ruled against teaching creationism, I don't think we are far from the time when our schools will be able to teach what creationists believe. So let us examine our hearts and repent of whatever impure motives we detect. Then we can help nonbelievers see Jesus more clearly.

Another way in which Christians and prior laws have been triumphalistic is in the criminalization of adultery and homosexual activity. Such activity is sinful and socially destructive, to be sure. Yet in the context of the twenty-first-century debate over homosexual conduct, I don't believe we should use law enforcement to stop people from homosexual conduct. It does not mean, however, that we should stop warning, stop preaching the holiness of God, or cease to encourage repentance. Nor does it mean that we should not protect children from the social effects of homosexual conduct—particularly same-sex unions. It is one thing to allow adults the freedom to act as they want and quite another to legalize same-sex marriage. Christian ministries that succor gays with AIDS while not compromising biblical teaching are probably more effective in spreading Christ's love and mercy than laws outlawing homosexual conduct. We need a spiritual solution, not a legal one, to the sinful conduct of men having sex with other men, although we most certainly must consider the best interest of children when same-sex couples seek to adopt. Whenever homosexual conduct begins to affect others, particularly children, we must take legal action. And in this latter area, we must fight for justice and mercy without erring on the side of triumphalism.

REAL VICTORY

In 1 Corinthians 12:12–19, we read that we are to cooperate with other members of Christ's body, under the command of our Head, the Wonderful Counselor. Paul describes how God organizes the body with a diversity of gifts and unity of purpose. Our identity, occupation or avocation, our gifts, spiritual weaponry, and heart for children all commend us to cooperative action. And we follow our Head! So part of our victory is working together in unity toward a common goal.

The Bible has many titles of God and Jesus that help us respond to Him as our leader, especially in times of spiritual battle—from Elohim, meaning "the strong one," mentioned "in the beginning" (Gen. 1:1), to "arm of the LORD" (Isa. 53:1) to "deliverer" (Rom. 11:26) to "Almighty" (Rev. 1:8). The evils of our day—lawlessness, abuse of children, injustice, terrorism, and more—are to be recognized as such, resisted, and defeated, while also recognizing that God is using them to equip us as more than conquerors. Ultimately, the Lord's objective in allowing these battles is to lead people to repentance and salvation.

Finally, victory has always meant being persecuted while living a godly life in Messiah Jesus (2 Tim. 3:12), fighting the good fight, finishing the race, keeping the faith (2 Tim. 4:7), and doing the Father's will, not our own (Luke 22:42). I hope we all will strive to receive this commendation from the Lord: "Well done, good and faithful servant" (Matt. 25:21). So collective victory does not mean part of the army escapes hardship or death, but it does mean the entire body functioning harmoniously under the leadership of Jesus.

Unify!

Is such coordination even remotely possible given the disarray, confusion, and infighting among believers around the world? Of course! It will take an act of God, but God is able. I doubt He would give such visions of unity and victory in Scripture to discourage us. Our objective is to understand how we fit into His body and be productive for Him, where He has called us to be. If we are already ministering where God wants us as a stay-at-home mom, a fashion designer, or an overseas missionary, we should continue where He wants us to be. But remember that the command to unify includes not only taking our assigned position, but also spacing ourselves next to—not crowding or distancing from—others in the same profession or life situation and then keeping in order when our Wonderful Counselor directs us to move forward.

Confused? If so, here are examples:

If you are a homeschooler, connect with other homeschooling believers to learn from and encourage each other. Teach the Constitution but teach it as having authority only as it is consistent with God, our highest authority.

If you are a marine biology teacher and the only Christian in your department, organize a Bible study with believers in the history or athletics faculty. Twice a year at your biannual

PHOTO COURTESY OF DISCIPLES FOR CHRIST

Students work together to rebuild a home demolished in Joplin, MO, after the EF-5 tornado in 2011.

professional conference, seek out other believers so you can arrange breakfasts at each conference to pray together and invite not-yet-believing colleagues to hear the spiritual journey of a Christian lawyer. You can find such speakers at any major city through the Christian Legal Society or Alliance Defending Freedom.

If you are a law student or lawyer, attend the Christian Legal Society annual conference to be edified and discipled. Or start a local chapter in your city or at your school if one does not already exist.

If you are in a retirement or nursing home, pray strategically, regularly, and fervently—especially as you send out Qi Yuan Day cards.

If you are in a church, find out where there's a need and fill it! One Chicago area church has one of their core values supporting a "culture of life." To this end, they send busloads of young and old every year to the March for Life in downtown Chicago—in January. Throughout the year, they support a ministry called Replanted, which seeks to support foster and adoptive parents and their children. Not only are these families given help, but the entire church family is involved in a variety of ways.

Get the picture? In God's economy there is never unemployment, only job vacancies waiting to be filled. But, you say, I haven't been called! Yes, you have. This book you have been reading is about engaging our system of laws to bless God's world—consider yourself called. In the 1980s, Francis Schaeffer explained that Western civilization had lost its worldview of Jesus as Lord of all, that Christians still viewed Him as Lord of "religion" but no longer as Lord of science, the arts, law, or politics, and that we had succumbed to an unbiblical bifurcation of spiritual truth and material truth. Consequently, our effective impact on our nation had been impaired. Schaeffer's analysis was correct then and sadly prophetic as we have ingested the toxic compromise of a man-centered rather than God-centered understanding of reality, including law. However, that can change if we all function as we are gifted in His body.

Which Path?

At this time in His story, we as followers of Jesus have before us essentially two paths. One path I describe as defensive and protective, epitomized by the reaction of Israel to a Philistine show of force at Gilgal while Saul was king:

> The Philistines assembled to fight Israel, with three thousand chariots, six thousand charioteers, and soldiers as numerous as the sand on the seashore. They went up and camped at Mikmash, east of Beth Aven. When the Israelites saw that their situation was critical and that their army was hard pressed, they hid in caves and thickets, among the rocks, and in pits and cisterns. Some Hebrews even crossed the Jordan to the land of Gad and Gilead. Saul remained at Gilgal, and all the troops with him were quaking with fear. (1 Sam. 13:5–7)

The other path I describe as audacious advance, epitomized by David's confrontation of Goliath:

> David said to the Philistine, "You come against me with sword and spear and javelin, but I come against you in the name of the Lord Almighty, the God of the armies of Israel, whom you have defied. This day the Lord will deliver you into my hands, and I'll strike you down and cut off your head. This very day I will give the carcasses of the Philistine army to the birds and the wild animals, and the whole world will know that there is a God in Israel. All those gathered here will know that it is not by

sword or spear that the LORD saves; for the battle is the LORD's, and he will give all of you into our hands."

As the Philistine moved closer to attack him, David ran quickly toward the battle line to meet him. Reaching into his bag and taking out a stone, he slung it and struck the Philistine on the forehead. The stone sank into his forehead, and he fell facedown on the ground.

So David triumphed over the Philistine with a sling and a stone; without a sword in his hand he struck down the Philistine and killed him.

David ran and stood over him. He took hold of the Philistine's sword and drew it from the sheath. After he killed him, he cut off his head with the sword.

When the Philistines saw that their hero was dead, they turned and ran. Then the men of Israel and Judah surged forward with a shout and pursued the Philistines to the entrance of Gath and to the gates of Ekron. Their dead were strewn along the Shaaraim road to Gath and Ekron. (1 Sam. 17:45–52)

David used five smooth stones, the anointing as king from God by Samuel, and at least six spiritual weapons:

- the name Yahweh Elohim Israel, "The LORD, the God of Israel" (see also Judg. 5:3; Isa. 17:6)
- the name El Shaddai, "God Almighty" (see also Gen. 17:1)
- truthful speech in the power of God
- divine power to demolish strongholds
- the sword of the Spirit, the Word of God
- faith

We are all familiar with the story of David and Goliath. As believers, we may feel like an insignificant shepherd boy facing a celebrated warrior. But let us remember that God uses the weak to shame the strong. God constantly used the lowly things of the world to accomplish His purposes to show that He alone is the one able to accomplish His purpose. And He has equipped us to do His work, to fight the battles before us. So what are our resources as we face the Goliaths of the twenty-first century? Here is a list of just a few, and more can be found in Appendix C:

- fellow believers, with whom we can unite and who can strengthen and encourage us
- churches, congregations, missionaries, and ministries worldwide
- the right to vote and the ability to inform other voters
- lawyers, judges, and law students who love God
- over a dozen organizations litigating for religious liberty (see Appendix B)
- Focus on the Family and other family-values organizations worldwide who can help us understand how to better care for children
- our Wonderful Counselor

So which path shall we choose? If you love God and those for whom Jesus came, I ask you to enlist as soldiers in God's army fighting legal battles. If you or your congregation are unsure of how to get involved, survey your talents and spiritual gifts, search your heart, ask our Wonderful Counselor to guide you, and consult with other Christians to discern the best way for you to participate in what God wants to do through the church. God has provided most facets of these spiritual resources to be best exercised corporately. If you are a pastor or church leader, or feel called to become a leader, then consider how one or more of these fields of opportunity can become a ministry for your congregation. You need to find the field of engagement where your fellow believers await to join forces. If you already know where God wants you, then call others to your side, square up, and move forward at His command.

A PARTING WORD

Dear reader, you have seen in this book how the legal aspects of Jesus' ministry, and the interaction and attitude He wants us to have toward the law and even lawyers, have been obscured or misunderstood. Jesus' desire during His days on earth and now is to use law to secure the rights of people so they can hear the gospel, to promote human flourishing through laws that promote the common good, and to advance His already-not-yet kingdom. If we are going to be faithful citizen-disciples in this world, we need to continually keep in view how Jesus taught, thought, and interacted with the legal establishment of His day and accept His challenge to do the same as His followers today.

Now, understanding how God's laws and precepts are the best plan for the flourishing of humanity, how we can be part of the legal process as citizens, how we can not only defend our own interests as Christians, but also be known for advancing the godly interests of others, let us prayerfully and vigorously engage! As we do so, let us remain joyful and hopeful in both victory and defeat. For we know what is partial today will one day be complete. What is left unfinished on this earth, including in our courtrooms, will one day be made right. "Look, I am coming soon!" Jesus says. "My reward is with me, and I will give to each person according to what they have done" (Rev. 22:12).

Amen and amen!

A SPECIAL NOTE TO PASTORS

As I have noted throughout this book, churches face serious obstacles today relating to the legal realm. Yet they need not fear, for numerous resources can be used to protect themselves.

It is highly recommended that churches adopt a clear statement of faith regarding human sexuality and marriage in their congregation, that churches clarify that weddings held in their congregation are Christian worship services, and that churches adopt a policy that clearly restricts the use of ministry facilities to the ministry's religious purposes.

Here are two helpful resources related to sexual issues:

1. "Protecting Your Ministry from Sexual Orientation Gender Identity Lawsuits" (adflegal.org/campaigns/pym), provided by Alliance Defending Freedom, which includes:

   • A "Statement on Marriage, Gender, and Sexuality"

- "Sample Standards for Evaluating Prospective Students"
- "Sample Handbook Agreements for Parents and Students"

2. "Church Guidance for Same-Sex Issues" (clsnet.org/ document.doc?id=852), provided by the Christian Legal Society, which includes:

- "Practical Legal Steps to Address Same-Sex Issues and Related Nondiscrimination Laws"
- A sample of church doctrinal language on marriage and sexuality issues
- A sample of church bylaws language
- A sample of a wedding policy
- A sample of a facility use policy
- A sample of employee handbook language

See also the Alliance Defending Freedom's website for helpful resources on freedom from government intrusion (adflegal.org/ issues/religious-freedom/church/key-issues/protecting-the-church/freedom-from-government-intrusion), which cover:

- protection from the Sexual Revolution's legal advance
- civil marriage licenses
- property taxes
- 501(c)(3) status

There, you can also find resources on how churches should navigate political and cultural involvement (http://adflegal.org/ issues/religious-freedom/church/key-issues/protecting-the-church/church-political-involvement), especially:

- elections
- voting
- legislation

These resources will help churches and their leaders understand better what they can and cannot, should and should not say from the pulpit so they don't jeopardize their nonprofit status.

In addition to knowing how to effectively protect themselves from liabilities, churches must educate their members on how to faithfully integrate citizenship and discipleship in a culture that is becoming increasingly hostile to communities of faith.

CHRISTIAN LEGAL ORGANIZATIONS

Read more about these Christian legal organizations to learn how you can participate in and support the work of advancing God's kingdom by fighting for justice and mercy. Most of these organizations fight legal battles for religious liberty and family values. Some, as their titles or websites show, are more narrowly focused:

- Acton Institute (acton.org)
- Advocates International (advocatesinternational.org)
- Advocates for Faith and Freedom (faith-freedom.com)
- Alliance Defending Freedom (adflegal.org)
- American Center for Law and Justice (aclj.org)
- Americans United for Life (aul.org)
- Becket Fund for Religious Liberty (becketlaw.org)
- Center for Law and Religious Freedom (clsnet.org/center/news)
- Center for Public Justice (cpjustice.org)
- Christian Legal Society (clsnet.org)
- Home School Legal Defense Association (hslda.org)
- Liberty Counsel (lc.org)

- Life Legal Defense Foundation (lifelegaldefensefoundation.org)
- First Liberty Institute (firstliberty.org)
- Mauck & Baker, LLC (mauckbaker.com)
- National Legal Foundation (nlf.net)
- Pacific Justice Institute (pacificjustice.org)
- Thomas More Law Center (thomasmore.org)
- Thomas More Society (thomasmoresociety.org)

I also encourage you to consider praying for and supporting organizations like Focus on the Family. While Focus, and the many other family-values organizations, is not strictly speaking a legal organization, their efforts lead, support, and reinforce defenders of civil liberties in manifold ways.

Here is a list Christian and faith-friendly law schools:

- Regent University Law School
- Liberty University Christian School of Law
- Cumberland School of Law, Samford University
- Campbell School of Law
- Ave Maria Law School
- Baylor University Law School
- Pepperdine University School of Law
- Handong International Law School

ADDITIONAL SPIRITUAL RESOURCES

As I have explained throughout this book, we must not rely simply on our legal resources in working to establish justice and mercy in our world. First and foremost, we must rely on God and employ the spiritual tools and resources He has placed at our disposal.

As you work to advance God's kingdom in impacting the legal system, remember that prayer is your most indispensable tool. And as you pray, remind God and yourself of who He is by invoking the different names and titles of God as revealed in Scripture:

- Yahweh ("I AM WHO I AM," Ex. 3:14), which means "to exist," and can be invoked when praying for issues like abortion and the sanctity of life
- Yahweh Jireh ("The LORD Will Provide," Gen. 22:14), which can be prayed as a reminder that God will provide all that we need, no matter the circumstance
- Yahweh Nissi ("The LORD is my Banner," Ex. 17:15), that God is our leader, who gives us strength and victory

- Yahweh Shalom ("The LORD is Peace," Judg. 6:24), that God is our peace and can bring peace to our world
- Yahweh Sabbaoth ("The LORD of Hosts," 1 Sam. 1:3; 17:45), that God is a mighty warrior fighting for us
- Yahweh Maccaddeshcem ("The LORD your Sanctifier," Ex. 31:13), that God wants to make us and our world holy
- Yahweh Ro'i ("The LORD my Shepherd," Ps. 23:1), that God is always leading us, His people
- Yahweh Tsidkenu ("The LORD our Righteousness," Jer. 23:6), that God alone is righteous and can bring justice to our world
- Yahweh Sammah ("The LORD is there," Ezek. 48:35), the Lord is always with us
- Yahweh Elohim Israel ("The LORD, the God of Israel," Judg. 5:3; Isa. 17:6), that our God has intervened in space and time to be the Lord of a specific nation
- Elohim ("strong one," Gen. 1:1), that nothing is impossible for God
- El Olam ("the everlasting God," Isa. 40:28), that the Lord is without beginning or end, He does not change, and He will be faithful to us

We can also pray the names and titles of Jesus, our Wonderful Counselor:

- "Arm of the LORD" (Isa. 53:1), who works to accomplish God's plan in our world
- "Blessed and only Ruler" (1 Tim. 6:15), the one who has ultimate charge of our world, even the legal system

- "Cornerstone" (Ps. 118:22), the one on whom we and all we do, even our engagement in the legal realm, are founded
- "Everlasting Father" (Isa. 9:6), ruler from all ages over all creation
- "Firstborn" (Rev. 1:5), the Son of God, equal in power and authority with the Father, who alone possesses all authority
- "High Priest" (Heb. 4:14; 6:20), who has atoned for the sins of the world and is continuously interceding for us
- "Image of God" (2 Cor. 4:4), the one to whom God wants us and all people to be conformed
- "Immanuel" (Isa. 7:14), the God who is always with us, even in our legal endeavors
- "Redeemer" (Job 19:25), the only one who can redeem our world, including the legal system
- "Son of David" (Matt. 1:1), the King who has come to perfectly rule Israel and our world
- "True Light" (John 1:9), who exposes darkness and injustice in the world
- "Governor" (Matt. 2:6), who watches over us and all our endeavors
- "King of kings" (1 Tim. 6:15), the supreme ruler of our world who will one day return to establish justice once and for all
- "Righteous One" (Acts 7:52), who knows how to live rightly before God and men, and who gives us the strength and grace to do so
- "Suffering Servant" (Isa. 53), the one who suffered for us and our world in order to bring justice and mercy to the world, and who is with us as we suffer in seeking to do the same

- Baptizer with the Holy Spirit (Matt. 3:11), who has sent us both the other Counselor and His gifts

As we engage the legal system at whatever level, we must always be intent on using whatever attitudes, attributes, or spiritual gifts the Lord has given us (see 1 Cor. 12:7–10; 2 Cor. 6:4–10) and on embodying the fruit of the Spirit (Gal. 5:22), so that we may represent Christ well to all those we encounter.

Of course, we must continuously study and meditate upon God's Word, speaking it to others whenever possible. Let us remember that God surrounds us with His angels, who watch over us. Fasting is a hugely beneficial practice that enables us to focus on God and become increasingly attuned to Him and His will for the circumstances in our lives (see Acts 13:2; 14:23).

As we discussed in several places throughout this book, God wants us to have the same attitudes toward His Law as exhibited by the psalmist in Psalm 119. Moreover, these attitudes will help us have the right attitude toward good human law and lawyers, that we may engage the legal system for the good of others and God's glory. Here is a list of just a few of the attitudes toward God's Law highlighted in Psalm 119 that we should seek to cultivate in our own hearts and minds:

- Obedience (v. 5)
- Hidden in heart (v. 11)
- Enthusiasm (v. 32)
- Longing (v. 40)
- Theme song (v. 54)
- Thanksgiving (v. 62)
- Delight (v. 77)

NOTES

CHAPTER 1: WOE TO YOU LAWYERS?

1. "Justice Byron White: Dissent from *Roe v. Wade* and *Doe v. Bolton* and their Progeny," *EndRoe.org*, http://www.endroe.org/dissentswhite.aspx#_ftn3.

2. Ibid.

3. Some of you may be thinking, *Wait a minute. Luke was a physician, not a lawyer!* Well, yes, he was a physician (see Col. 4:14). However, in *Paul on Trial: The Book of Acts as a Defense of Christianity* (Nashville: Thomas Nelson Publishers, 2001), I explain how Luke wrote Luke-Acts as a legal brief to defend Paul from charges pending against him in his trial before Nero.

CHAPTER 2: TURNING HEARTS TOWARD GOD'S LAW— AND GOD'S LAWYERS

1. "Who We Are," on *Alliance Defending Freedom* website, https://www.adflegal.org/about-us/who-we-are.

CHAPTER 3: LEGAL ADVANCES THROUGH WONDERFUL COUNSELOR JESUS

1. This humorous appellation for an "important person" derives from the British legal practice where the higher-ranking judges wore bigger wigs than the lower ranked.

CHAPTER 4: GOD'S SPECIAL PEOPLE

1. Emma Green, "Why Are Fewer American Women Getting Abortions?" *The Atlantic*, June 17, 2015, http://www.theatlantic.com/politics/archive/2015/06/american-abortion-rate-decline/395960/.

2. "Special Edition: Sojourners Presidential Forum," on *CNN* website, http://transcripts.cnn.com/TRANSCRIPTS/0706/04/sitroom.03.html.

3. Douglas W. Allen, "High school graduation rates among children of same-sex households," *Review of Economics of the Household,* vol. 11, no. 4 (December 2013): 635.

4. See familystructurestudies.com.

5. Paul Nyquist, Is Justice Possible? (Chicago: Moody, 2017), 107–108.

6. *Zelman v. Simmons-Harris*, 536 US 639 (2002).

7. See also, John Mauck, "Bible Colleges Shouldn't Need a State Seal," *Wall Street Journal,* March 19, 2015, https://www.wsj.com/articles/john-mauck-bible-colleges-shouldnt-need-a-state-seal-1426805663. If you want to inform your prayer in this realm of battle, you'll enjoy linking to this lawsuit, which we feel has been directed by our Wonderful Counselor: Complaint: https://issuu.com/mauckbaker/docs/20150116_complaint_w.attachments; Opinion: https://issuu.com/mauckbaker/docs/038_memorandum_opinion_and_order; Appeal: https://issuu.com/mauckbaker/docs/001-1_civil_case_docketed.

8. Michael Bloomberg and Charles Koch, "Why Free Speech Matters on Campus," *Wall Street Journal*, May 12, 2016, https://www.wsj.com/articles/why-free-speech-matters-on-campus-1463093280.

9. Judith M. Glassgold et al., *Report of the APA Task Force on Appropriate Therapeutic Responses to Sexual Orientation* (American Psychological Association: August, 2009), http://www.apa.org/pi/lgbt/resources/therapeutic-response.pdf), v.

10. See, for example, the studies of Joseph Nicolosi (josephnicolosi.com),or the Alliance for Therapeutic Choice and Scientific Integrity (therapeuticchoice.com).

11. For a sample of Jones's work see Stanton L. Jones, Mark A. Yarhouse, "Ex Gays? An Extended Longitudinal Study of Attempted Religiously Mediated Change in Sexual Orientation," presented at the Sexual Orientation and Faith Tradition Symposium; APA Convention, 2009; https://www.cedarville.edu/~/media/Files/PDF/Student-Life-Programs/Critical-Concern/Ex-Gays/jones-and-yarhouse-2009.pdf.

12. DVD available at ChristianBook.com (www.christianbook.com/such-were-some-of-you/9780964500082/pd/500084).

13. *Singleton v. Wulff*, 428 US 106, 118 (1976).

ACKNOWLEDGMENTS

When I agreed to undertake a book about Jesus and lawyers, I received an unusual confirmation from the Lord that this book would be a team project: a battle half serious and half fun. It certainly has been.

Consequently, I wish to thank team members at Mauck & Baker who typed and researched: Tracy Robinson, Mikaela Hills, and Stephanie Grossoehme. And thanks to my law partners, Richard Baker, Whitman Brisky, and Noel Sterett, and to associate Sorin Leahu, who also encouraged and supported me.

Then there are the editors at Moody Publishers: Duane Sherman, Betsey Newenhuyse, and Kevin Emmert. They cajoled, challenged, wrestled—prevailing and yielding as appropriate—but ultimately sharpening. Many legal insights came to me through my longtime friend Messianic scholar Daniel Gruber.

ABOUT THE AUTHOR

John W. Mauck (B.A., Yale University, J.D., University of Chicago Law School) is an attorney, speaker, and biblical scholar who partners with men and women to discover God's powerful solutions amid the pain of church splits, litigation, and reconciliation counseling. The most satisfying moments in his thirty-year career as principal attorney of Mauck & Baker, LLC occur when his work results in churches being given the right to build, thus allowing the gospel to be preached and lived. For John, being a lawyer is about serving God. John was a board member of Christian Legal Society for nine years, and is currently an Allied Attorney with the Alliance Defending Freedom. His book *Paul on Trial: The Book of Acts as a Defense of Christianity* was a finalist for the Evangelical Press Association book of the year. He has hosted a weekly Bible study for lawyers for over thirty-eight years and discipled many to become committed followers of Jesus. He and his wife of forty years, Rosemary, have four adult children and have been active in prayer and healing ministries at First Presbyterian Church of Evanston since 1983.

BE CAREFUL WITH THIS BOOK

the stories inside will change you

WHY IS JUSTICE SO HARD TO COME BY?

Is Justice Possible? explores the realities of pursuing justice in a fallen world. Author Paul Nyquist considers the biblical and theological foundations of justice; obstacles to justice in human society; practical steps for pursuing justice in political, personal, and public arenas; and the hope of true justice upon Christ's return.

978-0-8024-1494-6 | also available as an eBook

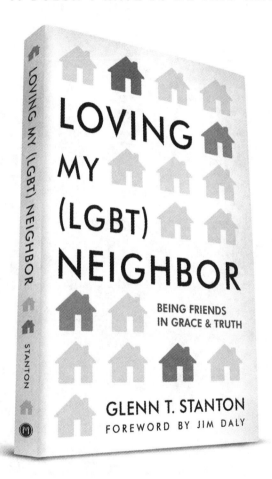